Puerto Rico Inside and Out

Puerto Rico Inside and Out

Changes and Continuities

FERNANDO PICÓ

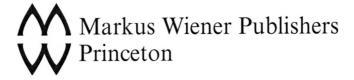 Markus Wiener Publishers
Princeton

For information, write to Markus Wiener Publishers
231 Nassau Street
Princeton, NJ 08542
www.markuswiener.com

Library of Congress Cataloging-in-Publication Data
Picó, Fernando.
  Puerto Rico inside and out : changes and continuities / Fernando Picó.
    p. cm.
  ISBN 978-1-55876-481-1 (hardcover : alk. paper)
  ISBN 978-1-55876-482-8 (pbk. : alk. paper)
  1. Puerto Rico—Social life and customs. I. Title.
  F1960.P54 2008
  972.9505'3—dc22
                                        2008024003

Markus Wiener Publishers books are printed in the United States of
America on acid-free paper and meet the guidelines for permanence and
durability of the Committee on Production Guidelines for Book Longevity
of the Council on Library Resources.

Contents

Preface ix

Part I. Through the Lands of Others: France 1
1. Nixon in Paris (Letter from Paris, March 14, 1969) 3
2. Cayetano in Paris (Letter from Paris, April 19, 1969) 6
3. On Exiles (Letter from Paris, June 24, 1969) 9
4. The Left Bank of Paris (Letter from Paris, August 22, 1969) 12
5. Letter from Santurce (August 27, 1969) 15

Part II. In the United States 19
6. The Washington March (November 21, 1969) 21
7. Progress Comes to Cayey (January 16, 1970) 25
8. A Requiem for Palo Seco (March 18, 1970) 27
9. The Puerto Rican Novel (March 24, 1970) 30
10. Stagnation 1970 (April 30, 1970) 33
11. The Grapes of Protest (May 15, 1970) 36
12. Hold-Up (November 6, 1970) 40
13. The Second Discovery (November 25, 1970) 42
14. Street Names and Punishments (December 31, 1970) 44
15. Previous Generations (January 13, 1971) 47
16. Conscience and *Conciencia* (January 27, 1971) 49
17. We Too Are Guilty (April 2, 1971) 52
18. On Good Memories (April 17, 1971) 54

Part III. An Interlude 57
19. Letter from Santo Domingo (August 18, 1971) 59
20. The Road to Puerto Plata (August 11, 1971) 61
21. The Birth of *Guimica* (October 16, 1971) 63
22. Parable of the Good *Pon* (November 2, 1971) 65
23. Letter to Doña Alvilda (December 4, 1971) 67

Part IV. Home and the Hues of Nostalgia 69

24. Doña Juana's Wise Man (January 3, 1972) 71
25. Remembrances of 1952 (February 19, 1972) 74
26. *Publico* Etiquette (March 31, 1972) 77
27. Nostalgia for Calle Loíza (April 23, 1972) 79
28. On Cantinflas (Letter from Madrid, August 16, 1972) 83
29. Utuado in 1900 (August 26, 1972) 85
30. The Art of Lottery Tickets (January 2, 1973) 87
31. A Sense of "Place" (April 17, 1973) 89
32. Professor McDowell (April 28, 1973) 91

Part V. A Time for Dissent 93

33. Revolt of the Trees (August 31, 1973) 95
34. The Value of Dissent (November 28, 1973) 97
35. *El Nacimiento* (December 8, 1973) 99
36. De Moca (December 29, 1973) 101
37. On Mosquito Nets (Letter from Cayey 1, January 25, 1974) 103
38. Bagatelle (Letter from Cayey 2, January 30, 1974) 105
39. A Gathering of Cousins (Letter from Cayey 3, January 31, 1974) . . 107
40. On the Importance of Symbols (February 6, 1974) 109
41. The Great Dominion of Canada (February 14, 1974) 111
42. A Rage of Referenda (September 23, 1974) 113
43. A Letter to Javariz (October 12, 1974) 116

Part VI. Past Imperfect 119

44. San Guibin's Day (November 28, 1974) 121
45. Chronology of an *Asalto* (December 26, 1974) 124
46. Bus Riding in Prose and Poetry (June 20, 1975) 127
47. Mrs. Ponce de León (August 7, 1975) 129
48. On Slaves as Lenders (September 20, 1975) 131
49. Six Thousand Utuadeños (December 15, 1975) 133
50. Voters of 1871 (February 9, 1976) 136
51. Don Samuel Quiñones (April 1, 1976) 138
52. Don Coco (July 24, 1976) 140

Part VII. In the Time of the Prodigals 143
53. The Prodigals (August 14, 1976) 145
54. Let's Not Confuse Training, Education (January 18, 1977) 147
55. Letter from Port-au-Prince (June 18, 1977) 149
56. The Coquification of Culture (July 6, 1978) 151
57. Titina and the 50's (January 27, 1979) 154
58. A Visit to the Lord of Chalma (July 18, 1979) 157
59. At Plaza Las Américas (October 17, 1979) 160
60. Grandpa's Story (November 29, 1979) 162
61. Teaching Methods at the University of Puerto Rico
     (December 13, 1979) 165
62. On Shoes as Flowers (May 22, 1980) 168
63. Scholarship in Puerto Rico (June 19, 1980) 171

Part VIII. Paris and Back 173
64. Monaco! Monaco! (Letter from Paris, June 27, 1980) 175
65. Alcuin or Merlin (June 30, 1980) 178
66. A Weekend Night in Paris (July 9, 1980) 181
67. A College for Prison Inmates (Letter from Paris, July 26, 1980) ... 184
68. Florencio Picó (August 28, 1980) 188
69. A Guaguita Driver's Binge (March 19, 1981) 191
70. Jorge Bauermeister (July 23, 1982) 194
71. Time for a Change (August 13, 1984) 197
72. Say Yes to People (June 2, 1987) 200

Preface

"I went to Puerto Rico last Christmas and they buy in supermarkets just like us." I was teaching Puerto Rican History at Fordham University in 1970-1971 and heard that reproach from one of my students. She had expected the island to be just like her parents had left it back in the 1950s. In those days, the second generation of Puerto Ricans in New York City tended to be somewhat dogmatic about what life in Puerto Rico should be like.

It was not until I definitively returned to Puerto Rico after more than twelve years of studies abroad that I understood that student's remark. I too had left the island late in the 1950's, and all through my years in New York State and Maryland and one year in Paris I had retained an idealized notion of what Puerto Rico was like. True, I had come down to the island a few times, but it was always for short whirlwind visits to family and friends. I had assumed that Puerto Rico had not changed, that I had not changed.

The shock of re-entry began in the summer of 1971, when I taught summer courses at the recently opened campus of the University of Puerto Rico in Cayey. For me, throughout the years of my absence, Cayey had been magical territory, where I had spent my summers as a child and where my grandmother still lived, on the coffee farm to which she had moved in 1911. I had not been prepared to see that the old agricultural society had crumbled, that no one was a *jíbaro* any more. The *jíbaros* had dominated the folklore of my adolescent years. They were those noble, emaciated, hardworking men and women of the mountains who defined the essence of our collective personality, or so I had been taught. No longer so. Emigration, industrialization, and urbanization had wiped out the *jíbaro*. Radio, television, and schools had extinguished the *jíbaro* talk. My uncle Jorge Bauermeister, who loved the old ways, urged me to write about that fading

ix

society, of don Vivian the healer and Lola la Pollera the gambler, and of the old hands who had worked on the coffee farms.

Thus, at the outset of my return home, I was confronted with two images of Puerto Rico, one, the fading world of the *jíbaro*, and the other, the militant scene of the second generation Puerto Ricans I had met in the Bronx. Curiously, both visions repudiated the new Puerto Rican society and culture that was emerging in the 1970's. When I started teaching European History at the main campus of the University of Puerto Rico in Río Piedras in 1972, I was startled to find that there was a generational battle brewing between the traditional professors and the new brash recruits to the faculty. The old members of the university establishment defended what was later called the Western canon, objective truths that could not be questioned, a certain formality of address and deportment, and crafty controls over students' activities. Since I had so recently been a student myself, I was surprised to find that what had been taken for granted at Johns Hopkins and elsewhere in the northeastern states in the 1960's was considered either radical or fuzzy thinking at Río Piedras in the 1970's.

Trying, like any non-tenured professor, not to attract undue attention to myself, I nevertheless wound up on the insurgents' side at the university. But cultural conflict was not restricted to life on campus. The Jesuit Order to which I belong was facing similar disarray, especially after Pedro Arrupe and the Jesuit General Congregation launched the order's commitment to issues of justice. In my own family, my nieces and nephews, impatient at the traditional Puerto Rican constraints on the young, were also charting their own itineraries. I felt caught in the middle of all these contests of will. Eventually I made two fateful choices. I started to spend time with my ailing grandmother, doña Alvilda, in her old house in the mountains of Cayey, and, when she died, in October 1974, I kept spending weekends there. Furthermore, in January 1975, I decided to put on hold my research on the French medieval clergy and started working on the social history of Utuado, a coffee growing municipality in the center of the island. Thus I turned my back on San Juan and on my previous academic research and spent weekends indexing notarial and baptismal acts, walking on the mountains, and writing.

Since my student days in France in 1969, I had combined doing research for my dissertation with writing columns for the *San Juan Star*. The columns were my window on the world. I had started as a columnist describing life in Paris, but now I was commenting on current affairs in Puerto Rico. Although the *Star's* readership was smaller than that of the dailies in Spanish, the professional classes tended to read the *Star* as well as the Spanish dailies. I was surprised to find out that one was reproached if one diverged from accepted ways of looking at Puerto Rican society. I had to learn to say things in a light way, to make readers laugh. Every now and then I threw in a "heavy" essay, but it was easier to make a point if one incorporated dialogue and appealed to fancy.

In the 1980's I switched to writing in Spanish and gradually abandoned my niche at the *San Juan Star*. Readership had changed, it had become more conservative and more fastidious, and I had changed, too, or thought I had.

These essays deal with continuity and change in Puerto Rico as I perceived it at the time. I am not sure that I still subscribe to all my observations (and that may explain the omission of some columns from that period), but I want to share both the joys and perplexities of that stage of my life. Only minor editorial changes have been made to the original columns, published on the indicated dates.

I am grateful to *The San Juan Star* and to managing editor Ronald Walker and his successors at the newspaper for having given my columns space on the editorial and opinion pages for so many years.

* * * * * *

I dedicate this book to the memory of my uncle, the geographer Rafael Picó (1910-1998), and his wife, professor Teresín Vidal.

Part I

Through the Lands of Others: France

1. Nixon in Paris

(Letter from Paris, March 14, 1969)

I was doing my dissertation research in Paris, and then Richard Nixon barged into my life. I shared the experience with San Juan Star *readers.*

On Thursday, February 27, a young policeman comes to see me with a summons. "Be at the local police station tomorrow afternoon, at 2:30 precisely." He bows—everybody here bows—and leaves.

I begin examining my conscience, as you would do if the same thing happened to you. What had I done?

Once when I was nine I had kicked a cousin on the shin and had not apologized. In high school I was on the same volleyball team with one of the present leaders of the Puerto Rican Independence Party. Here in Paris I had once suggested in public that the General might not be able to get the upper hand of the mushrooms-and-snails smuggling crisis with Switzerland. Somehow it all doesn't add up.

Friday, February 28, 2:30 p.m. "Here I am."

"Oh, yes, monsieur, we have summoned you here on account of the American President's visit. As you know, he arrives this afternoon. We would like to have periodic checks on you. Sign this register here."

"Why?"

"Orders, you know. We just follow instructions. We want the President to be safe, so that's why we are asking Puerto Ricans to come to local police stations five times during the weekend."

"That's an outrage, a humiliation!"

"Don't feel bad; we're not being especially hard on you. When President Tito visited Paris we asked all exiled Yugoslavs to do the same."

"First of all, I'm not an exile. Second . . ." But what's the use. The

3

man doesn't even know where to start looking for Puerto Rico on a map.

4:00 p.m. I go to the American Embassy and explain the situation to the Marine officer who receives me.

"For Pete's sake," he says, "are they doing that? I'll inform higher-ups about it."

"Could I leave this letter explaining the situation?"

"Sure." He clicks his heels and I go out.

6:00 p.m. Second check at the police station. I sign. "I have lodged a protest at the Embassy, you know."

The inspector smiles at my naïveté and pats me on the shoulder. "They won't do anything, you know. But at least you tried. Don't forget to come tomorrow."

I try to contact other Puerto Ricans to see if they have undergone this bizarre treatment, but I don't succeed. In the evening press I read that Nixon has called De Gaulle a giant among men.

Saturday, March 1, 9:30 a.m. "Ah, bright and early," beams the inspector. "You see, it's just a formality. We who lived under German occupation know how hard this kind of thing could get to be."

"I still protest. This is systematic discrimination. My American passport is as good as anybody's."

"Maybe you have done something." The inspector looks at me doubtfully.

I go back home and phone the Embassy. The operator gives me the Press Office, and I explain to a Midwestern girl at the phone what has been happening. "For Pete's sake," she says, "are they doing that? I'll connect you with the Security Office."

The Security Officer sounds bored. "For Pete's sake," he says (which gives me the impression that everyone in the Embassy staff is taught to say this phrase at each and every occasion), "is French security doing that? Well, well, I always knew they would go to extremes."

"Couldn't you see to it that this thing is stopped? This is an insult to the people of Puerto Rico."

"Yes, of course."

I explode.

4:30 p.m. "Ah, monsieur, it's almost over now. Then we can all forget about it."

"I won't. Could you show me the instructions you got on me?"

It turns out they only have my name, age, address, occupation, and one condemning word: "*Portorricain.*"

"This is absurd."

"Maybe you have decided opinions on something," suggests the assistant inspector paternally.

I have decided opinions, yes, but they all concern the 13th-century bishops of my thesis.

"By the way," the inspector says, "tomorrow we are closed, Sunday, you know. We'll have to ask you go to the main district headquarters at 12:30 p.m."

They discuss whether I should go by subway or by bus. "Perhaps you could walk. Good exercise." They shake my hand and wave good-bye.

The evening papers report that Nixon has praised the incomparable genius of the leader of the French people.

Sunday, March 2, 12:30 p.m. The district headquarters are across the street from the National Assembly. Two inspectors are eating sandwiches; they wave me in with a "*Bonjour!*"

I give them my summons.

"Oh, yes . . . where did we put it? Here it is. Would you sign here?"

I do, and ask whether I can write underneath a note of protest, but they say it's not done.

3: 30 p.m. "The President has just left for Rome."

More power to him.

2. Cayetano in Paris
(Letter from Paris, April 19, 1969)

I could interview my imaginary friend Cayetano, and he would say things I did not necessarily feel free to say. This is a sample.

My friend Cayetano washes dishes at a Left Bank restaurant, plays the guitar on the boulevards, and writes an interminable novel. Recently he was making comparisons between life in Puerto Rico and in France.

"There are quite a few similarities, you know. Take for instance the sense of old things. In New York when you say a building, a piece of crockery or a scarf is old, you mean it's time to replace it. In Arecibo, or Aibonito, on the other hand, when you say something is old, you are praising it. "That is an old house, *del tiempo de España,* or better still, "Be careful with that tray: it belonged to my grandmother."

He paused to sip the cheap Bordeaux he drinks and continued. "Do you remember when the Tree of Lies outside Río Piedras was cut down to make room for that intersection? Why, I believe more tears were spilled over that tree's disappearance that at all the funeral eulogies delivered under it. Well, the chestnuts at St. Sulpice Square here in Paris have been cut down and you should see how my concierge is upset. I think she'll actually vote *non* in the upcoming referendum on account of it."

"That's French logic for you."

"Funny you should bring up French logic. For that's another thing I find similar. You know how Californians or Midwesterners think."

"I don't."

"Well, when a Californian buys razor blades or a pen, he tends to buy a brand he recognizes. If it's well advertised, he thinks it's a

6

responsible firm with a lot of capital behind it; they won't sell you a shoddy product. Normans or Angevins here in France, on the other hand, think just the reverse: If they have to have advertisements, they must be trying to fool me."

"But people in Puerto Rico are much more used to ads," I object.

"What kind of ads?"

"Well, the regular ads. In fact, I thought that you believed that the way so many TV ads in Puerto Rico are dubbed straight from the national networks was a sign of how poorly advertisement was coordinated."

"But it is. Think of all those instant happiness ads, when a detergent or a deodorant solves the crisis of a whole life. That kind of ad works in the States because most people don't take them seriously; they look at the ad for its entertainment value and then remember the brand. But in Puerto Rico people's expectations are raised and of course find no satisfaction, so that in the end people mistrust all that genre of ads."

"And in France?"

"Here they make the same logical jump. If a canning company promises family happiness by drinking their brand of juice, it cannot possibly be good juice."

"What you're saying is that both Puerto Ricans and French are mistrustful. They don't want anybody to take advantage of them, so they have hellish agonies on the kind of light bulb they should buy."

"But it all comes from this Mediterranean logic. Take for instance the love for real estate and the tremendous real estate inflation in both Paris and San Juan. Or the tremendous spirit of competitiveness ranging from sports to academic achievement in both places. Or the emphasis on the power of the human will in both traditions. The readiness to feel insulted. The way political life revolves around given political figures. And finally the disregard in which non-lucrative professions are held there and here."

"What is the common premise?"

"None. But there's an individualistic logic behind all these things. The States is supposed to be the land of rugged individualism, but it's no longer true. You say something like hippie culture can't last or it's cheaper to buy a sofa at the neighborhood furniture store than pay it over a year at a department store and people arch their brows. Here in France everybody does things differently and there are 50 million opinions on what's best in a salad. As the General so well put it, it's hard to govern a nation where people eat over three hundred different kinds of cheese."

"Cayetano, I think you're getting Gallicized. Isn't it time you took the plane back to New York?"

But he just ordered another Bordeaux.

3. On Exiles
(Letter from Paris, June 24, 1969)

"Sitting by the streams of Babylon . . ." The literature of exile haunts Paris as it does any of the great metropolitan centers of the West. In New York it was O'Henry's strays and Willa Cather's success stories, Madrid knew the bitterness of Becquer's Andalusian recollections, and Dostoyevsky's Saint Petersburg brimmed with hopefuls from the four corners of the Russias. Paris, however, has been historically the city of strangers par excellence.

To this day, when the wind blows from the south people in the Beauvaisis still say: "The wind is coming from France." Considering that Beauvais is 50 miles away from Paris and has been practically attached to the central government of France, for better or for worse, since 1233, when that ill-starred count bishop, Miles de Chatillon-Nanteuil, was unable to put down a riot against the mayor of the city, it's not hard to imagine how heavily in exile provincial Frenchmen feel in Paris.

Rutebeuf sang the plight of the uprooted peasant's son, arriving at the university "to spend his father's last sou." The French kings themselves felt uncomfortable in the cosmopolitan river city and preferred the hunting lodges of the surrounding forests (lodges now known as the palaces of Vincennes, Compiegne, Fontainebleu, Saint-Germain-en-Laye and Versailles). The correspondence of the French Revolution leaders is thick with references to their own homesickness in this gigantic carcass of a city.

Gregoire dreamed of Lorraine, Arras's Robespierre did not feel at home even with his loyal hosts at the rue Saint-Honoré, and the bumbling Girondins never survived the charge of looking much farther than the spires of Bordeaux when considering the welfare of France.

9

The French elite has ever come from the obscurity of the provinces, settled late in life, if not confidently, in Paris, and never ceased deploring the lost charms of Colombey-les-Deux Eglises (De Gaulle), Villers-Coteret (Dumas) or Britanny (Renan).

If the French are homsesick in Paris, much more so the Spaniards, Portuguese, Algerians and Africans whom they import for the menial jobs without which this hand-operated capital would soon come to a standstill (and often does). They sweep the gutters every morning, punch the subway tickets, collect garbage, wipe clean the shop windows and stuff the moving vans with the fragile porcelain of millionaires giving up the city for its lush suburbs. They are underpaid, live in miserable attics and hundred-year old firetraps with little or no heating, and they seldom see their children get ahead. Work with dignity and integrity—these are fine words; they apply to the sons of small shopkeepers who memorize, with mamma's help, the Latin declensions and the algebra formulas that open the way to success. If you are a Spaniard and demand better living conditions, you are ripe for deportation.

The French live in blissful ignorance or indifference of aliens'conditions in France. A recent survey showed that 20 percent of Africans working in France get tuberculosis. "Ah," said triumphantly an acquaintance, "you see, they come and infest our nation!"

"Pardon me," said a wiry young Belgian present, "but the same report says that they get TB after they have been in France for an average of 18 months."

"My friend," said the older man, "if you are implying that we mistreat them, please tell me, how are conditions in their own countries when they come to France? Surely nobody forced them to come over."

It is strange, hearing that echo here in Paris, the petulant complaint of the native resident. I had heard that before, in New York: "If Puerto Rico is so beautiful, why do you come over?" It's the chant of the megapolitans when they hear us, grumbling nomads of the sunny countries: "Go back, go back, you don't belong with us, scarf-and-gloves people, Fifth Avenue shoppers, Westchester commuters." A tropical fraternity of exile links that Senegalese woodcarver who sells his mahogany masterpieces on the sidewalk of boulevard Saint-Germain and those British citizens of Indian descent born in Kenya, men without a country whom the British government has left stranded, suspended between London and Nairobi airports, with us, Puerto Ricans, roaming from city to city, clutching a passport that assures us a welcome anywhere but where it was issued.

It's not a question of nationality, or of economics, or of pragmatic politics, as the three political traditions in Puerto Rico have insisted, but of the old social distrust between the men who love walls and those who have the sun for their heritage.

4. The Left Bank of Paris
(Letter from Paris, August 22, 1969)

This was my valedictory column, saying goodbye to Paris after a year's residence. I was due in Woodstock College, Maryland, to start studying theology. I flew down to Puerto Rico via Madrid and from there went to Maryland.

Of nights, when you walk along the banks of the Seine, or better still, down boulevard Saint-Michel, thronged with students and peddlers of wire jewelry, you know that this is the perfect city. So much life and energy, and all the forceful engagement of lights and color, the cafes, where you can sit for hours watching people percolate into boulevard Saint-Germain, speak of freedom and health, and rather cavalierly dismiss money as the center of life. On the sidewalks of the Left Bank, barefoot students and their girls play the guitar or draw chalk madonnas. Sometimes, when it is not too hot, an elderly violinist plays classical music near the subway exit by the church of Saint-Germain-de-Prés. One night a Spanish girl sang on that spot, and there must have been more than 300 people listening to her. From the back coins were tossed over the heads of the crowd, and she sang, one after the other, 15 songs.

What there is of cynicism in the City of Lights resembles the dregs of Greek coffee. If you stir the cup it will come to the surface and embitter your mouth. You mustn't drink too deeply, just to the edge of sweetness, and leave the rest. People here will tell you that the spirit of Paris is being throttled. Since Pompidou's election, new signs have appeared in all the subway stations reminding all that the writing of graffiti carries heavy penalties according to a city ordinance dating to 1942. The irony of it. Paris was occupied by the Germans then. For students, who can't legally assemble or publish some of their papers, a well-scribbled phrase on a subway wall had been the only means of conveying their contempt for the regime. In any case, graffiti won't die; if anything, they will become sharper.

But politics is only part of the scene here, and it absorbs the energies of relatively few. Ideology is much more important. On the Left Bank you spend interminable hours discussing the principles you believe in and bringing out all the subtle nuances that distinguish you from your friends. The idea of holding exactly the same views as anybody else, be he president, wife, Marx or Cohn-Bendit, would startle a Parisian. If you are a leftist—and I have never heard anybody in France call himself a rightist—there are hundreds of denominations for your stance, and these in turn are modified by words like "neo," "pure" and "orthodox" and by hyphens (once I was told somebody was a Freudian Christo-Marxist).

While Germans' chief anxiety seems to be health, here in Paris one is more concerned about one's "name." If someone calls you a bourgeois nihilist, you stay awake whole nights thinking of the appropriate slur to cast back. To be recognized or snubbed on the street, to refuse a handshake, or to be invited to this or that get-together becomes a crucial operation. "Next October," a scholar I know confided, "I am scheduled to give a talk in Strasbourg. The only problem is that my rival [and he mentioned the name of somebody who just received an important distinction] will be there giving another talk. Inevitably, we'll meet face to face. I am sure I'm not going to shake his hand, but I still don't know what to say at that moment. It better be good because people will repeat it afterwards."

The movies would make you believe that there is little room for pettiness on the Left Bank of Paris, that you can stroll forever, meeting people with happiness halos who will share their vintage wine with you. But the last refuge of innocence and candor in the Western World, should it thrive on the Left Bank of Paris, would be accessible only on payment of a hundred francs plus service. It's not the people you meet who are greedy, but the proprietors behind the scenes, the landladies, the hereditary bookstore owners, the bankers who wear their Legions of Honor to strut through the salons of fashionable hostesses—they have their paws on the Left Bank, exploit its charm, and wring every centime they can from the continuous supply of visitors.

If you are dreaming of walking barefoot on the rue Saint Jacques bring plenty of band-aids. What is liberating can be painful. If you must wear sandals, better become a monk, immured in one of those stout 12th-century abbeys that dot the countryside, far from Paris's Left Bank, already excoriated by Bernard of Clairvaux in the 1140's. There is La Trappe in a green valley of Perche, or Saint-Wandrille, or, in an even further reach into the past, Saint-Benoit-sur-Loire. For Paris and these forgotten bastions of asceticism have historically complemented each other. The refugees from one have flown into the other. Fugitive medieval clerics wrote Goliardic poetry in Paris. There was too the student of 1200 who reportedly heard from his window in the Latin Quarter the song *"Time is going and I have done nothing."*

"He experienced a change of heart," says the contemporary moralist, "and abandoning all things set out for a Cistercian monastery the very next morning."

5. Letter from Santurce
(August 27, 1969)

Santurce is my own native ward, that part of the city of San Juan that grew fast in the first half of the 20th century and afterwards has been shrinking steadily. The natives of Santurce call themselves Cangrejeros. This is a record of my return to the barrio after a year in Paris.

Parcel out the time you spend here in between stays abroad and allot the shortest quarter of an hour to the pumpkin patch that grows all over the place where your neighbor's house stood in Santurce. And who's my Neighbor? You are out-parabled by the Good Samaritan story, all-time preacher's favorite, puzzling any Cangrejero who returns, prodigal son, Odysseus-like, weary of twisting his mouth to say the four foreign sentences that get him a meal. For Santurce, as remembered, was a place of shady neighborly streets where you knew and trusted everybody and shared friends' joys and their panic every time a hurricane poked its nose over the Leeward or the Windward Islands-one could never figure out which.

Remember those early 50's hurricane bulletins? What maps of the Caribbean, year after year, were stored for future reference-the hopes offered by last-minute switches in direction? Who ever remembers the storms that missed? But the boarding up, the patient storing of china, the offering of shelter by those who themselves were hardly secure, all the camaraderie of neighbors sipping black coffee while waiting for the Weather Bureau to say at 3 in the morning that we were to be spared once again. These are memories of another Santurce.

For who's your neighbor in Santurce now? All these gigantic *condominios,* where people have people over at the cocktail hour; the parking places, steaming by day and desolate by night; the Avenida

Norte, ripping a whole parish apart; the legendary future, but now desolate clay, of Avenida de Diego; and Ashford Avenue, no longer belonging to us Cangrejeros, but to a world dreamed up by strangers who read stranger-than-life fiction: They do not fit in that picture of the 50's, that tenuous hold on a share of life's glory that was Santurce's winning of the baseball pennant.

There was Manolo and his wife, Petra: the good Lord one year heard their prayer-promise and gave Santurce the pennant. For it, they had promised to go a whole month to mass at 6 o'clock in the morning. San Jorge parish didn't have any mass at that hour. Since they had to distribute papers early in the morning, they fulfilled their promise by kneeling in front of the locked church doors every morning at 6.

There was Christmas Eve in the Calle Loiza, with people coming over to the drugstore for their last-minute shopping and advice. "And what should I buy, *doña* Lolita? Last year it was soap, but she has soap."

They have cut down trees everywhere and taken down houses, the married sons and daughters have moved to the *urbanizaciones* (subdivisions) in Río Piedras, and the parents have remained, salvaging memories out of the wreck, telling tourists which buses to take and appeasing their own fears. Fear of robbery. Brothers who steal, spare the old man's wallet and the widow's knickknacks; it's too fragile a world and no one cares.

Santurce is acquiring the tough resigned face of the Bronx. "What's the Bronx good for?" "To go to Manhattan." There are the beaches, but they are no longer the old neighborhood places where kids built sandcastles over a week's period. Make an act of faith, then, in the future Santurce, rich and busy.

But remember the stranded poor-not the statistics the new generation with its doctorates and library shelves dishes out, but the grocery store messengers who lingered to play pranks on the cooks, the lottery ticket vendor who promised us fantastic wealth every week, the chronically unemployed and unemployable drifter who repaid a cup of coffee with stories of pirates' buried treasure, and all the lonely people, like in the Beatles'song:

All the lonely people,
Where do they all belong?

In old Santurce, by the open door of the bar next to the movie-house, in the heat of the afternoon, waiting for the fabled horse Camarero to win his 50th race.

Part II

In the United States

6. The Washington March
(November 21, 1969)

The Washington Moratorium was a well organized but costly effort to mobilize hundreds of thousands of people to protest the war in Vietnam. Recently arrived from Paris, I was studying first year theology at Woodstock College, the Jesuit seminary in Maryland. José was actually a classmate, Gustavo Preston, since deceased. We were recruited as marshals.

How does it feel to be at the center of a half-million people protest march? How organized is it? What measures of safety and protection are taken? The best way to find the answers is to become a protest marshal. With José, a Fordham University alumnus from Bayamón, now residing in the Baltimore area, I discovered it was easy to assume the rank and the duties.

It was 8 in the morning. "By the authority vested in me by the people of Vieques, I declare you Marshal of the Washington March." We tied handkerchiefs on each other's left forearms and stood at the end of a line outside Ebenezer Baptist Church. With casually asked questions we found out from the other marshals what our duties were to be. This group was the Wedge. We would march at the head of everybody and protect the personalities who were leading the protest.

We boarded a chartered bus that took us to Ford Street in the Mall. There we linked arms and formed a half circle. We were on.

First came Eugene McCarthy, with whiter and thinner hair than the campaign posters of '68 would have suggested. The aging politician. The networks brought out their cameras and microphones and we cleared space. What was remarkable was his ability to concentrate on each question. He didn't let his eyes stray. Then he read a statement.

21

Lashing out at the new draft program for 19 year olds, he carefully built up to an attack on the Nixon administration. When he finished, the approval from the gathering crowd was wild. Some took up the magic chant, "We want Gene!" but the march organizers quickly shouted over the microphones, "Peace now, peace now!" and the crowd picked up the organizers' slogan.

The marshals were given American flags to carry. "You're at the head and people should see that the march is patriotic." Then the march started and we hit Pennsylvania Avenue. No clouds, and a wind that chewed each bone in your body. It was the photographers and cameramen who properly led the rest; they walked backwards, or rather jumped, like sad court jesters. We were instructed to let them come through our ranks whenever they pleased. "It's important to make them happy."

The march down Pennsylvania Avenue was exhilarating. The barbarian neoclassical facades of the Federal buildings are softened with the perspective you get from the middle of the avenue. Most of the people on the sidewalks were sympathetic. At some corners Nixon supporters had signs, but there were three policemen for each one of them. They had had their own day on November 11 and most had stayed home today.

When we reached the grounds of the Washington Monument we picked our way to the speakers' platform, where our job was to protect the scheduled speakers. It was a long wait before the rest of the crowd arrived. And what a crowd! Wherever your eye reached there were people, coat-and-tie people, poncho and fedora people, people dressed, painted, befeathered in all the colors of earth, old, young, and in arms.

Lunch was rather informal. Somebody gave me half of his peanut butter and jelly sandwich, somebody else passed around chocolate Easter eggs, and I got a sip from an orange juice container someone from behind handed me. A guy sitting in front of the marshals started tossing apples in the air and hands reached out for them from everywhere. Another guy tossed potato chips bags and oranges. Nobody had to go hungry; it was a huge meal of fraternity, Renan's version of the miracle of the loaves and the fish.

When everybody was sitting and the music and the speeches were about to begin, a contingent carrying Viet Cong flags filtered forward, the Weathermen, the humorless, doctrinaire faction of the Students for a Democratic Society. They stationed themselves all along the perimeter of the platform and refused to sit down.

The marshals, two deep, stood up. We were all tense. Would they try to rush the platform? Instructions were passed out. We linked arms. The Weathermen taunted us, "That's it, follow your instructions. Sheep!"

We were sheep, but some of the speakers were "bourgeois pigs." They heckled Howard Samuels, the upstate New York industrialist, and Senator Charles Goodell. While the crowd laughed along with Dick Gregory's barbs at the vice president (Agnew), the Weathermen shook their fists.

More instructions were given us. "They'll try to rush when Senator McGovern speaks. Stand firm. Crouch a bit, if they shove; it's the best way to stay balanced."

While tension grew I thought of the television watchers looking at the Vietcong flags around the platform and wondering about the march. Would it ever come home to them that there was this rift among the marchers? A tiny, militant band of bullies playing on the nerves of the organizers could cause havoc. What if they broke through us? Would anybody of the stature of McGovern ever again participate in a mass meeting like ours?

When McGovern's turn came we tightened ranks. Behind us another string of marshals was added. The Weathermen started shouting obscenities at the senator. He ignored them and continued his speech, and all of a sudden they were quiet. They weren't listening, but they realized the crowd was not with them.

Then Pete Seeger sang and he led all the hundreds of thousands in the simplest song of peace:

All we are saying
Is give peace a chance.

The crowd began to disperse. The Weathermen were heading for their next confrontation at the Justice Department, where they succeeded in being tear-gassed. As we drifted away, José looked at the American flag that had been handed to him at the beginning of the march. "Only for peace, I tell you. Here I am, an *independentista,* and I end up carrying an American flag for a whole day."

7. Progress Comes to Cayey
(January 16, 1970)

*My maternal grandmother and uncles lived on the mountain over Cayey,
El Torito. Cayey has always figured significantly in what I write.*

The four-year regional college and the coming of the expressway
will no doubt bring new prosperity and life to Cayey. As the last *jíbaros*
leave El Torito for the cities and the continent, San Juan people scramble for panoramic villas on the hills of Guavate. An impressive shopping center is rising on what used to be grazing meadows on the out-
skirts of town. By 1980 the rural days of Cayey will be a memory.

While the town bustles, the hills empty and die. You look down with
binoculars at the new roads and housing projects. Can it be the same
one-church town of Moncho Frade the painter—don Moncho, who
painted brown angels on his huge *Our Lady's Assumption* long before
the poem *Píntame Angelitos Negros* became fashionable?

It's a time for salvaging memories. The emptying hills will soon be
mute. Like bulldozers lumbering through banana groves, the meaty
indifference of *Sanjuaneros* coming over for their bridge and whisky-
and-soda Sundays stamps out the voices and the stories of the people.
The *jíbaro* who stays becomes the housekeeper of villas, the typical
man who roasts the typical pig to impress the city man's invited
tourist. Would that Abelardo Díaz Alfaro took to El Torito before it
speaks no more.

For stories of the old days still circulate. You can still hear about
Lola *la Pollera,* who on payday played cards with the sharpest of
working men. To safeguard her earnings she carried a double-edged
knife. Her luck was legendary. Legendary too were the powers of don
Vivian *el Curandero,* who healed ailments in the bones and joints of

horses and men. "He knew the layout of joints," my uncle Jorge says. "He would approach a horse, feel out the bad leg, make a sign of the cross over it, and then apply pressure on some point. And it worked. People from everywhere would ask for him."

There was the man in a white cowl who showed up one day and built himself a hut on a hillock. He had a long beard and a prophetic look. A forerunner of The Last Times, he neither toiled nor spinned. People who hardly had enough to eat themselves would bring him lunch. He rarely spoke but just squatted and looked down at the valleys. That was twenty years ago, when meditations on the beyond and hippiedom had not been mass-produced. He was a happy man. I think he stayed five or six years undisturbed and undisturbing before the town sent somebody up to take him to a mental hospital. A woman had complained that he gave the evil eye to her children.

And there was Minga the cook. By rights she should have sat at the lexicographers' meeting just held in San Juan. Nobody ever spoke like Minga. She made soup of chicken legs and intestines which she advertised as *alimentosa*. She would recall the *domplines* she had eaten on the coast. "Dinner is plop-plop," she would announce to family and guests, meaning that the vegetables were boiled. Minga was a great judge of character, but her enmities were fierce. On a departing gossip: "She must have been *sangrigordita* when a girl." Somebody bewitched was *inducío,* and somebody tricky *mañudo.* Minga looked forward to the Last Days, when there would be more men than women, and the men would come chasing after her.

"Minga, how can that be? There's nothing like that in the Gospels."

"Well, I heard it from a wise and holy priest, a Spanish missionary, and that's just what he said, and if you don't believe me, so-and-so was there too and is my *aseverao.*

Minga, Lola *la Pollera,* Vivian *el Curandero* and the man in the white cowl have long left El Torito. The coffee groves are being cut and the *guaraguaos* shot down with mail-order rifles by teenage Sanjuaneros.

8. A Requiem for Palo Seco
(March 18, 1970)

In a second-hand bookstore in Baltimore I found one of those rare bargains that make browsing worthwhile. For $2 I purchased the two volumes of William S. Bryan's *Our Islands and Their Peoples,* a turn-of-the-century presentation to the American people of the newly acquired American possessions. Volume 2 bravely starts with a photo of "A Native Hut and Family—Near Coamo, Porto Rico":

"This hut and the family that occupies it are above the average of the dwellings of the peon class and the people who inhabit them. The houses are merely intended as shelters from the rain, and are rarely entered at any other time. At night all the family sleeps on the bare floor, without bedding or furniture of any kind."

The account proceeds with picturesque explanations of the ways of the natives. There is a plentiful supply of pictures of the Santa Isabel-Coamo-Aibonito area. Throughout the tone is missionary. There is so much that the conquering nation can do for this benighted people who have come under its aegis! But one must be patient:

"It is natural to suppose that for a generation or more to come the men to be elevated to office will come principally from the old, influential Spanish class, and that they will be largely influenced by the ideas of government that prevailed during the Spanish era."

It is Volume 1, apportioned unequally between Cuba and Puerto Rico, that introduces one to San Juan around the turn of the century:

*"The average denizen of San Juan is a silent but most eloquent expo-
nent of habitual somnambulism. He appears to be perpetually wrapped
up in slumber; I have sometimes thought his ambulatory hours, if anything, the more restful, because therein he need never so much as dream
of having to work."*

Now, while all the obvious things could be said about this pictori-
al account of Puerto Rico around 1900, how it caught half the population with its pants down, how it reeks of colonialism and pater-
nalism, it may be worthwhile just to look at the places it shows. Take
Palo Seco near Cataño, for instance. On page 273 of the first volume
there is a gorgeous one-page picture of an unspoiled beach. When I
saw Palo Seco last December the water was black and the sand stank.

A few pages afterwards there is a picture of a river in Bayamón.
Would you believe that it looks like the kind of river you'd love to
have a picnic by? Then there is a picture of Guaynabo's main square
that makes it look like the ideal tourist trap. A few pages after that
there is the church of Río Piedras and—gasp—there are gardens in
the square and a real, honest-to-goodness hill in the background. A
picture of Arecibo's square sends you back to seventeenth-century
Spain, lovely in its severity. In Yauco there's spaciousness and serenity; the center of town has been designed for people to stroll and enjoy
themselves.

What have we done to all those lovely spots, beaches, riverbanks,
hills, gardens, town squares? Think before you get on your rhetorical
hobbyhorse and blame a) politicians, b) capitalists, c) ignorant parish
priests, d) the population explosion.

There are no cars in these pictures, no people wearing coats and
ties out of Puritan compulsion, no weight watchers, no billboard slogans and ads, disposable cans, bottles and plastic containers, no
frozen foods or loudspeakers. There is little pavement (Sanjuaneros
are people of the *losa*).

There are fears and anxieties—about storms, plagues, hunger, gossip, evil eyes, demonic seizures, and powerful men. But these people
whom a hundred remedies, spells and promises to the Virgin cannot

save from the indignities of sickness, misery and death love the land and care for what they have made and built.

For Palo Seco, as it is now, shorn of all loveliness, only a handful of fishermen speak. Few care to listen, They are so utterly typical, the displaced locals who cannot accommodate themselves to progress. But if this is progress, the stench, the pollution, the insensitivity of people elected to care, make sure to take plenty of pictures for your grandchildren to look at in fifty years. They may find it amusing to see trees and green hills and people not wearing gas masks.

9. The Puerto Rican Novel
(March 24, 1970)

For as long as I have known him Enrique has been writing the Puerto Rican novel. Not just any novel, not a good story for you and me to read on a quiet Sunday afternoon, but the Puerto Rican novel. All I know about it is that it will have thirty-seven chapters and that the first and the next-to-the-last have been written.

On meeting Enrique at a party you ask how the novel is. Then you ask him about his wife. The novel, he will tell you, is doing fine. It just needs a bit more texture, a bit more episodic context. You, of course, will nod knowingly, and ask the fellow on your left whether he has done any fishing lately.

We all know that Enrique's novel will never be written. To this day nobody has learned whether it is in Spanish or in English, whether it takes place in Puerto Rico or outside it, whether it's a romance between a Spanish conquistador and a Taíno girl or the story of a flat tire on the road to Caguas.

Having met people engaged in writing the definitive Mauritanian and South Dakotan novels, I have become skeptical about the chances of the Puerto Rican one's ever appearing. At this display of cynicism, nationalist friends stagger. "Surely," they say, "after having seen *La Carreta . . .*"

"What does it prove?"

"That there is a theme," they all say in chorus, "a great theme waiting to be used."

The alienation of man from his land. Uprooting. Fine, but hasn't this sort of thing been done over and over again in other languages with other national awakenings? Isn't the whole nineteenth century staggering under the weight of tomes about the good peasant lad who

30

loses his soul in the big city?

Perhaps, of course, this horse has to beaten dead before Puerto Rican literature can move into the seventies. The Great National Awakening. Some electric novel about a young lawyer preferring poverty in exile to the degradation of becoming rich through bonds. Flashbacks to Spanish days, slaves toiling at a sugar mill, beautiful heiresses swooning with love for the fatherland. Hollywood would love it.

Great fiction has never been written by catechists, whether of nationalism, socialism or the divine right of kings. Somebody, naturally, is bound to object that *Uncle Tom's Cabin* was written with the express purpose of getting slavery abolished. Of course, if that's your idea of great fiction, stop me dead. But the real reason why Puerto Rican literature, however flourishing it may be within the confines of local coteries, is that it isn't genuinely popular. It's written for other Puerto Rican writers to read. You pour out your soul proving that you are a Father of the Country. Your peers will detect all the clever allusions and symbols of imperialism you have planted throughout the text. No one else will care, and that, the writer will attribute to ingrained colonialism.

The wider Puerto Rican public does read, but since it's not interested in the literary games of the literary establishment, it turns to American and Spanish bestsellers. Or, increasingly, to films. It won't react to a Puerto Rican novel until one appears that is rooted in Puerto Rican life as it is lived today.

There is a theme waiting to be seized: social change. If it's used to preach textbook doctrines it will merely bore. If it's charged with stereotyped *jíbaros* exchanging their innocence for dollars, it will never get off the ground. And if it's conveyed in the language of Castile or Colombia or Mexico City, it will be never be Puerto Rican. The Spanish of San Juan, and not that of Jayuya, the people of Santurce, not T.V. *jíbaros*, the afternoon rush hour in Hato Rey, not Llorens Torres' Collores.

The trouble with our revolutionary writers is that they keep heading back to the nineteenth-century womb. They are too busy writing for each other's published and unpublished anthologies to listen to the people of the *urbanizaciones.* So long as the current literary establishment rules, we won't have a Puerto Rican's Puerto Rican novel.

10. Stagnation 1970
(April 30, 1970)

In the spring of 1970 it seemed to observers in the States that the perennial Puerto Rican status question was about to be resolved by an option for statehood, since Luis Ferré's New Progressive Paper had won the 1968 elections and was actively promoting the cause of statehood. The New York Times's *Tom Wicker came down to take a look and wrote some columns. I was in Maryland at the time, and this was my reaction.*

That Tom Wicker should write columns on Puerto Rico for *The New York Times* should be a portent for the middle-aged, American-educated technocrats who want to run our island society. He doesn't sympathize with the Ferré generation. He is telling the coat-and-tie commuters of the East Coast that the presidential vote for Puerto Rico might not be the best thing. He has challenged the Puerto Rican gerontocracy.

In the States, however, the liberal establishment will file away the Wicker columns for citing at cocktail parties in the unlikely event that Puerto Rico's status might be discussed, sandwiched, perhaps, between remarks on the price of Malagasy vanilla and arguments about the California grape boycott. For the East Coast doesn't care anymore about Puerto Rico than about the Pope's visit to Sardinia.

What may be significant at all about the Wicker columns is that the Washington- based journalist has got sucked into the status debate. For like the kitchen sink, everybody and everything that comes to Puerto Rico these days ends up being sifted through the status question. And that, perhaps, is an index of the provincialism that the island has attained in recent years. Our status has become everything.

It's Don Quixote's doing that the world should be peopled again

33

with knights and giants and maidens to be rescued. Long has it pored over its books, this elderly generation of anti-Communist crusaders and their money-grubbing Sancho Panzas, and now it is set on this errand to solve the status question. Wherever they go, the dull litany of island politics replaces the hundred and one urgent questions to be examined. All outsiders must submit to the ordeal, be instructed in the secular mythology, which gods were against us and which for when that first ship headed for Guánica. Whether they are state-hooders or not, the don Quixotes turn the world upside down, calling shepherds abductors and innkeepers statesmen. For them Castro lurks in every corner, and in the face of Castro communism, the status question must be liquidated.

So it's bad that Wicker has come to repeat the status pros and cons, a journalist between two flights worried over subtler issues. All mainlanders who stay in San Juan long enough take sides. The sadness lurks in the misplaced assumption that by interviewing "key people" you might get to know what the man on the street thinks. For the man on the street doesn't think anymore, he watches the pageant of the Manchego *hidalgos* and shrugs his shoulders. The status jousters have become like competing brands of aspirin.

The service Wicker could have rendered would have entailed seeing the island with new eyes. He could have attacked the issues beyond status: the loss of the tropical environment, the unfulfilled aspirations of the chronically unemployed, the critical shortcomings in education, the decline of the small towns, the loss of traditional family values, the quagmire in which the local Catholic Church is moulding, the emergence of a new, idealistic generation that yearns for the excitement of supporting righteous causes and can't change flat tires. But these are the developments that don't get thought about because people are too busy discussing the new secretary of justice or the latest university resignation.

In short, the more we talk about status to visitors, the likelier we are to make them believe that what matters to us is which flag or flags are flying over El Morro. But the people you meet in the squares of Cidra and San Lorenzo, the people who play the horses three times a week, or shop in the new commercial centers, or visit second cousins on Sundays, or put flowers on their mothers'graves once year may talk about status as one may talk about heaven and hell, with much conviction and little desire to get to the crossroads.

All these earnest conversations about who we are and what our goals are as a people don't fill either stomachs or imaginations. There may be no physical or cultural starvation in Puerto Rico, but there is a great deal of hunger resulting from poor diets: rice and beans and status twice a day.

11. The Grapes of Protest
(May 15, 1970)

I was scheduled to defend my doctoral dissertation in history at Johns Hopkins University on Monday, May 4. The prospect of spending a weekend waiting for the defense was bleak; at Hopkins they can ask you in your defense about any topic, and some people were known to have skimmed through encyclopedias in sheer panic. So when Jeff Donnelly invited me to participate in a three-day march in support of Cesar Chavez and the Farm Workers Union, I immediately accepted. This is what happened.

The 200 marchers for César Chavez's grape pickers' union started out from the new town of Columbia in Maryland's Howard County on Friday, May 1. Fifteen hundred arrived at the Agriculture Department in Washington on Sunday, May 3. It was the last of the integrated marches, the last of the joyous demonstrations before the anti-Cambodia invasion rallies of the beginning of May.

At the head there was a banner of Our Lady of Guadalupe carried by two *braceros*. The American, Mexican, and Filipino flags followed (the Puerto Rican would be added on the last day). A freedom bell donated by a British union came next on a handcart. Six people pulled the cart and three people steered the handles. Then there were dozens of red flags with the black eagles of the grape pickers' union. The whole procession was tied together with music:

De colores, de colores
Se visten los campos
En la primavera.

36

It was great to sing out on such a spring day, walking through semi-rural Howard County, waving at cars, chanting the Chavez cry: *Huelga! Huelga!* On such a day a 30-mile pilgrimage seemed made to order. And if you were cynical (but then what were you doing there?) you'd say that the suburbanite housewives, the clerics, the hippies, the fat labor leaders, all the Chaucerian pilgrims had come out to march for the grape pickers just for kicks. A thing to do in May.

Then the sun gets hotter, the going rougher, the singing dies out. On the gravel alongside Route 29 we plod. Now that the cameramen and the reporters have evaporated, it is no great glory to carry the handcart with the bell. Shirtless toil. "Keep to the right," the marshals shepherd us. "Slower. There are stragglers in the back." There are rest stops. An ambulance is waiting there each time. "Any blisters?" Not yet. And so on to Burtonsville in Montgomery County. As we enter the town a man comes out of a bar: "My son just came back from Vietnam; you bums should be sent there." No answers. Further on a woman stops her car: "I have stopped buying grapes ever since I left Minnesota." Applause.

We have an evening meal at the local Methodist church. Singing on the lawn; weariness; heat. The minister consulting with his son: "Is the iced tea holding out?" He purrs contentedly, going from group to group shaking hands. An announcement: "We have a medic here to take care of all blisters." A first-class march, with Band-Aids and sun lotions.

A Quaker high school provides quarters for the night. Trying to sleep on the floor of a barn full of theater props and 50 other people, you start wondering about your sanity. "How did I ever get into this?" You have about fallen asleep when it's morning.

On the road again through the Washington suburbs. It's Saturday morning and the golfers are out. People in cars wave and make the peace sign. The Mexicans in the march are happy. "It wasn't like that when we marched from Delano to Sacramento. Sixty-seven of us started out and it was hard. But when we arrived there were 10,000 of us." The march, then, is a reenactment of the great 300-mile march. The songs, the flags and banners, the slogans belong to a liturgy of commemoration. Only César is still missing.

Lunch on the roadside. The sun pommels you. The medic keeps checking for blisters. An old lady from Rockland County in New York can barely walk. She stays to the end.

On again, up hills. The gravel is fierce on your shoes. Spirits are high, though. For most of the Mexicans, this is their first trip to Washington. We enter Silver Spring shouting "Boycott scab grapes!" The Saturday afternoon shoppers are transfixed. Is Mrs. Mitchell right and the Russian revolution has arrived?

The evening meal is at a park on the Washington city line. You rest against a tree gobbling tepid food. But accommodations are better— four of us are put up for the night at a Chevy Chase residence. A shower, pillows, a bed.

On Sunday an open-air mass under the rain at which Chavez finally appears. He steps out of the crowd and delivers a low-key homily on the grievances and aspirations of the grape pickers. Then we line up to march. I am in the middle of the line; César comes up: "Can I step in here?" "*Como no.*" Down Georgia Avenue and 16th Street we march together.

Lunch is at an Episcopalian church, Saint Stephen's. I sit on the sidewalk with an elderly, black truck unloader from Mississippi who tells me he joined the march when he saw us coming in the morning. Beside me a housewife from Queens wonders how soon she can leave for New York: "I have a protest tomorrow morning at Cardozo High School."

Last stage of the march. We pass by the White House; someone starts shouting, "Nixon eats grapes." It spreads, it grows in fervor, conjuring visions of the unpopular president recklessly devouring vast quantities, seeds and all. The tourists flock to take pictures. Then on to the Agriculture Department. The platform is a pickup truck; one by one congressmen, labor leaders, clergymen come to pledge their allegiance to the strike. Most moving is Willard Wirtz, President Johnson's secretary of labor. Last of all, César speaks—again matter-of-factly, straightforward. No rhetoric, no fat, just solid punches. The Department of Defense has helped the growers by buying non-union grapes. It must stop. The crowd cheers.

It's all over. You say goodbye to weekend acquaintances and hitch a ride back. Thirty miles doesn't seem that long anymore. You know that people you like, back home in Puerto Rico, here in the Baltimore-Washington area, will keep buying grapes, without looking for union labels, without a thought for the exploited Mexican-American farm hands. The hippies, the housewives, the labor leaders have tried to win the strike by dramatizing the boycott, but you know that the public still eats the grapes of indifference.

12. Hold-Up
(November 6, 1970)

There was a time when we liked to call New York City a barrio *(ward)* *of San Juan. It seemed then that everyone had to do time in the Big Apple before settling down again in Puerto Rico. I stayed on the Upper West Side of Manhattan from August 1970 to December 1971 while I studied theology and taught history.*

Mike is a college senior at Fordham University in New York. He had just stepped off of the university campus at 8:30 at night two and a half weeks ago when three young Puerto Ricans came up to him. One of them pulled out a gun. "Do you have any money?" As a matter of fact, Mike only had a nickel on him. "Well, that's no good," they said, "we need more." They turned around and walked away.

"Hey," Mike called out after them, "what do you need the money for?"

The guy with the gun came back. "For a friend of ours. He's been high and needs dough."

"How much do you need?"

"I don't know. Anything we can get."

"How are you going to get it?"

The fellow with the gun was silent.

"You mean you'll try to hold up somebody else?"

"We've got to get the money."

"But it's no good just going and picking on somebody else."

The upshot of it was that Mike went to friends in the university, got 10 bucks, and came and gave it to the guy with the gun. In the course of the conversation Mike found out that the Puerto Rican had dropped out of school. "Now, that's no good," Mike said, "you'll never get a job that way."

"I don't want to go back to school," said the Puerto Rican, whom we shall call José.

"Well, perhaps you can do something you want to do."

"I don't know," said José, "I thought once of being a Marine."

The other two fellows were getting impatient waiting, so Mike gave him his telephone number. "If you think I can help you, call me."

Well, about three days ago José did call. "I've been thinking," he said, "I spoke with the Marine recruiter, but he said I couldn't read English well. They give a test you've got to pass."

"Perhaps you ought to practice reading. I tell you what, I'll coach you."

So Mike went over to José's tenement house in the South Bronx and met José's whole family. They received Mike with typical Puerto Rican hospitality. Of all of them José knows English best.

Mike has started coaching José in reading and in English composition; it is hoped that José will be ready in a few weeks to take the Marines' reading exam.

"What's really rich in this whole story," Mike's roommate told me, "is that Mike is really antiwar. Imagine that! Coaching someone in reading so that he can join the Marines!"

Of all the mugging stories I have heard in New York these past few weeks, this is my favorite.

13. The Second Discovery
(November 25, 1970)

I was teaching Puerto Rican history at Fordham University while I was studying theology at Woodstock College.

Now there are two Puerto Ricos in New York, and the difference between them is not political or social, not one of language or religion, but one of style, of age, and of commitment. Nowhere was the contrast more evident than at Fordham University's Puerto Rican celebration of Discovery Day. Julio Montserrat, who was until recently one of the top educational figures in the New York City public school system, drew catcalls from a group of some 200 Puerto Rican college and university students. Pedro Pietri, a young, unshaven, casually dressed poet, had them on their feet cheering. If Puerto Rican congressman Herman Badillo had come—and he had been slated to come—he too, like Montserrat, would have been booed. They don't believe in Badillo, these angry students: "He only speaks Spanish when he campaigns, he belongs to the system."

Believe me, brothers and sisters who read the editorial page in between gulps of coffee down there where the nights are short, it's a new world. All those textbook words—"minority groups, low-income housing, equal opportunity, service program, civil rights"—man, they mean nothing. Like you are two payments behind on your living room furniture and the man is coming to get it, and all those phony salesman smiles—*Aquí se habla español*—now mean that you are trash. So, Mrs. Rodríguez, Jesus loves you more than you will know. Bible preacher thumping in some storefront service, and you pray to this saint or that, and then the landlord has your things on the sidewalk, roaches and all, and it's winter. And you grow up in this, you

42

see, the welfare lady asking patronizing questions, and checking on your mother's husbands. And in school the young, stupid teacher who can't pronounce your name, and so you grow up misspelling it, until you know better, and if you are lucky and hit a high school where you survive four years, you are chewed up by Pocahontas, the Bill of Right, and the second act of Macbeth. Drop out then. Or a college basketball scholarship, if you are not too short. And the Irish cop, who is a friend of the parish priest and gets free meals in the delicatessen, he checks on you and searches you and bullies you, and one day you call him pig, and he takes you away in the car and the people watch.

No, I did not write the above, I pieced it together from what I heard at Discovery Day celebrations. That is the scene today. The older generation of New York Puerto Ricans, with their baggage of rural memories and their penchant for "adapting," doesn't speak the way the young ones do. If correction officers in juvenile delinquency schools, who preach the civic virtues in Family Court cases, had been there, they would have learned quite a bit about how the young identify with Puerto Rico, resent being patronized, and dream the wild dreams of youth.

I have seen a correctional institution in New York State where Puerto Ricans were forbidden to speak Spanish. I know of a home for homeless youngsters where the counselors are required to know Spanish and scramble to learn the basics of the language, and the kids can't spell their homeland's name. I have talked with the kind of people who don't miss first nights at Lincoln Center, and they are sick with politely disguised prejudice.

The first generation of Puerto Ricans in New York put up with all the nonsense and choked with gratitude for not being run over by limousines. The second generation is angry, is electrified with rhetoric the Black Panthers use, and has nothing but contempt for the "ins," wants nothing short of the millennium.

14. Street Names and Punishments
(December 31, 1970)

After twelve years away from the island, except for brief holiday visits, I found out how much San Juan and its metropolitan area had changed. Riding buses was one way of discovering it.

Puerto Rican Dickens, wherever you are, surely you must have ridden on the back of buses to listen to what people say and to look at all those new subdivisions that the devil hatched in the interim between two administrations. If so, have you taken bus no. 11 through Río Piedras? Its route makes a map of St. Paul's missionary journeys look simple. It winds its way along streets that the driver himself must have discovered and asked his friends at the bar to name.

One wonders, for instance, how they came upon Sherman Street. Perhaps a diehard Puerto Rican nationalist, reasoning that Sherman was the destroyer of Atlanta, and Atlanta the site of one of Pedro Albizu's prisons, thus subtly honored the late leader. There is, too, Adams Street, which probably was a response to some urge in Boston to have a De Hostos Street. Or perhaps at the Public Works Department they have run out of street names and, having tried a few numbers here and there (with "southwest" thoughtfully attached, to give you the feel of Washington), decided to filch names from American history textbooks.

Belfast and Louvain, Glasgow and Bologna, it is hard to think of European cities not honored with a street name in San Juan. Why, aside from a couple of Filipino names, is Asia so underrepresented? No Tannu Tuva Street, no Kabul Avenue, no Kuala, Timbuktuo, or Luanda, much less Owerri, Addis Ababa, or Tanna. Perhaps it's more prestigious to live on a street named after a decaying Spanish provin-

44

cial bishopric than one honoring a brand new country. There is, too, the question of spelling and sound, those *mb*'s and reduplicated *k*'s . . .

It is magnificent to see, too, almost every possible dead Puerto Rican, Spaniard, and American recalled with a street name in the metropolitan area. All professions and parties—well, almost all—and all periods of history; Indians who may have never existed; soldiers who died in other peoples' wars; governors best forgotten; writers whom nobody who doesn't have to has read these past 50 years—they all have their streets. And 50 years from now, somewhere in Comerío, where cows happily slumber under bamboo trees, our current crop of politicians shall be running into each other in concrete regardless of party or persuasion, all because Public Works needs names for its streets.

Nosing its way within the merry maze of streets, bus no. 11 picks up generous numbers of people here and there. Your no. 11 people are not like the grim and earnest passengers on the Río Piedras-San Juan route, nor are they tired out and sullen, like those on bus no. 2 (Barrio Obrero-Villa Palmeras), nor are they reserved and fidgety about pocketbooks, like those of the Calle Loíza. No. 11 people, especially towards midmorning, are natural extroverts who know how to enjoy a bus ride and have good, pleasant conversation along the way.

And what were they talking about? Alas, poor politicians who polish your every sentence and make careful distinctions between your position of today and that of the day before yesterday, they were not talking about you, nor about the economy, nor about the cultural value of *areytos*. They were not talking about furniture bought in shopping centers, either, which was a relief, for I had started to believe that people talked about nothing else. On bus no. 11, people talked about what the best way was to punish children.

"The best way to punish them," a San Patricio grandfather maintained with vigor, "is a four-inch thick belt."

The opinion in the back rows was divided, an old Santiago Iglesias lady agreeing with him, and a young Altamesa girl dissenting in the name of humanity.

"Miss," said the San Patricio grandfather, "we were 12 at home and it was the only way."

"As for me," said a Plaza Las Américas mother, "I say the sooner they grow up the better."

And the bus rode on.

15. Previous Generations
(January 13, 1971)

They had told me in Cayey that Pepe Díaz had been brought to New York by his oldest daughter, and they had frowned. When would he play the *cuatro* now, he who had played from Three Kings' Eve all the way through the *octavitas*. God had made him to drink and sing in the open air, and tell tall stories, and work in coffee groves from 6 in the morning to 4 in the afternoon. And now he had gone to New York. What dirty streets must he be looking down on, Quebrada Arriba wondered, and how cold it must be and how gloomy the people.

"For you mustn't misunderstand," they said. "He was getting old and his daughter worried. There the doctors are close at hand. Yet what is that old man going to do up there? That's no place for him."

No place for the old, that pea soup of a city where anyone can disappear and be forgotten. Yet the old are leaving in droves from the island, brought up there in hopes of fatter welfare checks and the company of their immigrant children. Nothing left on the island to do but reminisce about the good, hard days, the times when one was young and picked coffee in the cold November rains.

"Prepare me a *ligaito*, for I'm off to work." To clear the coffee groves of *ortigas* in preparation for the harvest, to work at 2 in the morning on a tobacco *rancho*; no easy times those. And yet, you see, to be able to remember those days, to lean over the counter at a Latin grocery store in New York and say proudly, "You know, there were days I worked 12 hours straight with just a couple of breaks for coffee," that's something.

The sons and daughters don't understand. "Those days are over, *papi*; you were paid very little, you lived in a terrible place. Now you are with us; we have a television set, you can go to the movies."

47

And the elderly go to the movies on weekday afternoons, so that they won't have to stay alone in their apartments. Or they will get together, where their children won't hear them, and they will talk about hurricanes and wakes and brawls they have seen, and what was the fastest way to pick coffee.

"Now my late wife, she could do an *almud* in a half hour."

"A half hour? Impossible," the chorus protests.

"Oh yes, she could. You see, she was left-handed. Left-handed people pick coffee faster."

"Now, what stories are you telling . . . there's no difference."

"There is, I swear. She had tremendous balance, too, my woman had, and could pick from two trees at the same time."

And they brag about the plantations they came from. "Now, that was the best coffee there was. The governor himself would come to drink that coffee, it was so good."

But the immigrant sons and daughters interrupt: "Don't be telling people we came from the hills. After all, we lived in San Juan before we came up."

The grandchildren are worse, for they don't even get embarrassed, they are just bored and turn the radio on.

People asked me in Quebrada Arriba to give their regards to Pepe Díaz, and they gave me no address. "He's up there with his oldest daughter," they told me, "and see if he still plays the *cuatro*. He was real good at it."

One can just hope that he has bought a ticket in the million-dollar New York State Lottery. "And may that rambunctious Lady Luck, who loves to upset things, bring him a million dollars and bring him back to Quebrada Arriba, and may all who have been condescending to him eat their livers, amen."

16. Conscience and *Conciencia*
(January 27, 1971)

When I came to Puerto Rico for the holidays, it struck me that people weren't as concerned about the moral issues of the Vietnam War as in the States. Seeing that there was not much sympathy for conscientious objectors, when I returned to New York I plunged into the Oxford English Dictionary *and other assorted references and came up with this column.*

There are English and Spanish cognate words that are so similar that one easily believes their meanings to be identical. Take 'conscience'and 'conciencia', for instance. If you look up either in a dictionary, you expect the other one to be given as the translation. But do they mean the same thing when used in the respective languages?

Both 'conscience'and 'conciencia', like their cognates in French, Italian, and Portuguese, came into popular usage through theological manuals. At the root of them all stands the Greek *suneidesis,* which previous to the coming of Christianity had been in common usage among Stoics and had been given by them a Latin equivalent, *conscientia.* As it circulated in the Mediterranean world before Saint Paul, *suneidesis* basically connoted an awareness, what we call today *consciousness.* When the Stoics talked about a special kind of awareness that was sensitive to moral categories, they restricted *suneidesis* to apply to the faculty of a man who knew right from wrong.

The early Christians took the same word as their vehicle to express their awareness of what was right and what was sinful. Yet in the writings of Saint Paul, the word acquired a double meaning, for it began to denote not only the awareness but also the interior judgment of the moral value of what an individual had done. By the sixteenth centu-

49

ry, European cognates of *conscientia* had been coined to represent both meanings of St. Paul.

Conscience was well established in the English language by the time of the Reformation. It had come from the continent in the thirteenth century to supplant the Middle English 'inwit', a word that expressed not only the interior awareness of right and wrong but also the inclination to judge one's actions. Then the religious controversies of the Reformation were unleashed, and although both traditional senses of *conscience* were preserved, in the popular mind the 'awareness' meaning became uppermost.

In Spanish-speaking countries, on the other hand, the stress on individual sacramental confession, with its *examen de conciencia* as a preliminary requisite, resulted in the more frequent use of the judgment meaning. It also gave the word the coloration of 'memory', so that it became more frequently applied to past acts. Thus, in popular usage in Puerto Rico, to have a *mala conciencia* doesn't mean a lack of awareness of what is good or evil, but rather the remorse for having done something evil. *Conciencia* for us also connotes thoroughness, as when people say something was done conscientiously, *a conciencia.*

At this point, of course, it may be asked, what difference does it make? Surely the whole thing is a fine point? Well, take a conscientious objector (or, as I heard it in San Juan, *objetor de conciencia*). In Puerto Rico, seven years after the Vietnam War exploded as an international issue and provoked the greatest debate on a moral issue in the States since the abolitionists, conscientious objectors are the targets of popular reproach. To have a conscience that is sensitive to the moral implications of war means very little to most people, because the moral value esteemed is to have a *good* conscience, a clean conscience. You can keep your good conscience so long as you don't do anything wrong.

The conscientious objector, on the other hand, is not just interested in keeping his *conciencia limpia*. He is exercising his human faculty—and his constitutional right—to evaluate a moral issue and take a stand on conscience. In the States he is understood by a wider sec-

tion of the public, on account of what 'conscience' immediately connotes. In Puerto Rico he lacks the sympathy and encouragement of
his fellow citizens, and especially of the establishment, because they
can't get away from their utilitarian notion of *conciencia*.

17. We Too Are Guilty
(April 2, 1971)

Now that one guilty verdict is in and the fact of the My Lai massacre is legally established, it may be proper to assess our role in the massacre. It may, of course, shake comfortable armchair-consciences to speak of "us," of the uninvolved adults reading newspapers thousands of miles away from the events, uninterested in what has happened from day to day in that distant country.

But it is precisely the uninvolved and indifferent who made My Lai possible, the Garden Hills professionals who equated any opposition to the war with treason, the Hato Rey executives who accused of communism and subversion any one who dared question the legality or the morality of the military operations in Vietnam. The antiwar militant who doubted and compromised, the busy housewife who had no time for such questions, the respectable civic or ecclesiastical leaders who wanted to give no offense, the prudent and the peevish, the timid and the brash, the indolent and the cynical—we all have some bloodstains not easily washed away.

It would take such little effort to shift all the guilt on the military— just as it would be easy for the military to make William Calley the scapegoat. But as American citizens (and regardless of our status preferences), that army is our army and no belated disowning, no fine distinctions can dissociate us from the events at My Lai in March 1968. The massacre was the logical conclusion of the body count and the promised coonskin on the wall. Decades of anti-Communist indoctrination, of the glorification of violence, and of the hushing of dissent prevented our soldiers from resisting barbarous orders. They called it pacification.

In our collective efforts to out-Americanize the Americans and be more hawkish than the Pentagon, Puerto Ricans have become insensitive to the great moral issues of our times. If independentistas feel tempted by the above to feel self-righteous, let them remember that they too may have failed to loudly disavow violence, and insofar as they have condoned the rhetoric of bloodshed, they have become possessed by the same gut hatred and frenzy that was unleashed at My Lai. No, there are no escape hatches from which one can emerge innocent, for the antiwar march, the petitions, the letters to Washington, the earnest discussions at the cocktail hour, the smug denials of any consent to the war were unable to silence the guns of My Lai.

The war goes on, blindly wiping out villages with bombs. Our church leaders oppose abortion, but they speak in whispers about the burning alive of children and old people. Our veterans love to parade behind the flag and dress up in uniforms, but they shirk the harder patriotism of opposing this brutal war. Our politicians make nuanced remarks regarding their positions on the status question, claiming that they can exert no influence on war policies, but they are afraid that their names may end up in FBI files and their constituencies evaporate.

Nixon may worry about opposition in Boston or New York City to the war, but he need not worry about San Juan. Dumbly our draftees come forward for induction and the quotas are filled and everybody goes about his stipendiary duty. The coffins come back, the volleys of honor are fired into the air, and the mothers are given medals to show to visitors.

In other days there may have been cause for pride in such sacrifices—but these days one may ask, what for? Why should a Puerto Rican go to the other side of the world and shoot babies and torture fellow human beings and then come back maimed or psychotic? Yet we keep condoning the process, asking for time ("The war will end soon") or more facts ("It may be Hanoi propaganda"). Let us remember My Lai.

18. On Good Memories
(April 17, 1971)

There was a wave of nostalgia sweeping over the island in the early 1970's.

A while back in one of these columns, mention was made of the orange-colored Cayey-Guayama bus in the early 1950's, when the ride was full of good conversation, story telling, squealing pigs, bundles of flowers, sacks of oranges, sons, drama, and occasional swishing of blades. Since then, memories of those days have been coming to the fore, and I have found a surprising number of people who shudder at the idea that the early 1950's have passed on into history (statistics, content analysis, anthologies, guidebooks, and all the other things that fail to contain our childhood).

Take, for instance the word *pepelucazo*. We're in the second half of the ninth inning of the last game of the Santurce-Caguas island championship series. The game is broadcast by radio (no television yet). There are two outs. Santurce is down by a run and has one man on base. Its next batter up is relatively unknown, a Dominican called Pepe Lucas. Next instant the neighbor next door, a Santurce fan, hollers down the length and breadth of the street, "He did it, my God, he did it, a miracle." The *pepelucazo*, the necessary homerun in the extreme situation, gives Santurce the series.

And do you remember the visits to seven churches on the eve of Good Friday? I guess they are still made by some people, but nothing like then. It was a social occasion, when long-lost acquaintances were met on the steps of the cathedral or on the way to the *Capilla del Cristo*, which was only open on that day. In the churches, flowers, profusely veiled women and statues, unwilling children, second cousins asking in whispers about older people's health, candles sweating in dark chapels, sacred incense, incredibly long prayers, fervor, and frivolity.

What has happened to that great occasion, the seeing off of a relative at the airport? Now, my friends, we are down to the immediate family, but back in the early fifties a trip to the States meant the mustering of the clan, cousins and uncles, in-laws, employees, friends, servants, and neighbors. A three-month trip to Spain called for tears and orchids, ominous predictions, masses in the parish church, and "Notes" on the society pages. If you were a student and going to Europe until you finished your degree, there were traffic jams on the way to the Isla Grande Airport.

There is still quite a lot of visiting of the sick in hospitals, which shows that not all good things pass away, but it's nothing like it was twenty years ago, when new babies were peered at by processions of acquaintances, and young mothers were smothered in roses. The date of the mother's homecoming from the hospital was the subject of long diplomatic discussions, and baptisms were Homeric gatherings, so that when the simultaneous christening of several children was introduced, the church would be bursting with humanity.

Much has been said recently of the disappearance of different kinds of street vendors and their calls and refrains, but not enough can be said about the *dulceros*. They carried huge boxes on their heads. When they heard him children would run indoors in case their mothers hadn't noticed. "*Mami*, the *dulcero* is here." Then they would stand around expectantly as the *dulcero* displayed the most mysterious and delicious-looking pastries.

There are fewer *astromelias* planted these days. By some old houses you can still see them, probably untrimmed for years, but you don't find many of them in the *urbanizaciones* (subdivisions). Ungainly, unpretentious shrubs, they don't seem to fit in with lawns. But Santurce 20 years ago, when the *astromelias* were blooming and shaking in the wind—that's a period picture.

I'm old enough to remember one trolley car ride with my grandfather, but my first political reflection in life was that a city that got rid of such magnificent, thrilling things as trolleys couldn't possibly be perfect. Adults explained what having trolley cars meant to traffic, but it was the kind of thing grown-ups would say.

Shopping in Old San Juan? Well, where else, really. It was an expedition, a treat for children, a thing not done impulsively. Everybody shopped in Old San Juan. At Christmastime you had to elbow your way down Calle Tanca. Now you go there and meet some of the old people, always wanting more parking spaces and expressways. But it is luxury goods, art objects, restaurants, antiques, avant-garde shows, musical instruments, and that line of goods that suit the changed situation. Before the bay and the charm of the old city are destroyed with a bridge, somebody ought to take a look at what other metropolises have done with their old centers—Georgetown, Greenwich Village, and the Latin Quarter are good examples. You go there to get something you can buy only there.

And, to come full circle, the same applies to the remembered past.

Part III

An Interlude

19. Letter from Santo Domingo
(August 18, 1971)

After teaching summer school in Cayey, I went with a fellow Jesuit, Kirk Reynolds, to visit the Dominican Republic for the first time. Although it is only 45 minutes away by plane, the Republic, as people in Puerto Rico call it, was then far removed from our view. At that time, roads were still elementary and the country was just starting to fix things up after thirty years of governing by General Trujillo.

"Do you have any coffee?" the man asked the airline stewardess.

"Yes," she said readily. "But the machine is broken."

Latin reluctance to say "no" is ten times more evident in the Dominican Republic than in Puerto Rico. That's why so many visitors from San Juan to the recent *Festival del Merengue* found it hard to accept the reasons given for the disregard of their hotel reservations. The puritan "yea, yea, nay, nay" has gotten to Sanjuaneros, inducing us to accept affirmatives at their face value.

We have forgotten the art of always saying "yes" even when "no" is meant. "That's honesty," somebody is bound to remark, but it is also a sign that we are more at ease dealing with propositions than with persons. If the Dominicans' habit of saying "yes" may be unnerving at times, it also implies an acceptance of you as a person, not as a cipher.

"Is this the road to Guaymate?" I asked an old man at La Romana. He could have said "yes" and let it go at that, but clearly that did not suffice. He launched into a description of all the major sights on the road—the stretches of young sugar cane, the gray-green pine trees, the blue-coated sugar mill houses, Guaymate itself—and ended wishing us a happy and safe trip. Guaymate was 20 minutes away, a drab

59

place in anybody else's eyes.

In Puerto Rico we are becoming accustomed to mute signs and symbols; you can go around the island without opening your mouth, with no personal contact whatsoever. In the Dominican Republic that is manifestly impossible. Stray for a moment from any of the three good roads and you will be stopping again and again to ask for directions. That is a great excuse for meeting people.

They will tell you about the rains last year washing away the pavement and the bridges; about the cranes and the cement mixers that have passed by; about the new church down the road and the park that has changed names three times; about the earthquake last June; about the village where the children go to school and the grocery store, the gas station, the *ceiba* tree that mark a turn-off point.

"And the road to Ramón Santana, is it good?"

"So-so, but you will pass with God's help."

"But is there no other?"

"No other. But there are some good parts." And they talk again about the rains and make each stone and tree and cloud come alive with some personal attribution.

The road to Ramón Santana is for those who need not get there. If you travel on it, leave behind those half-baked notions of comfort, safety, and speed that have been giving tourists ulcers and turning their travels into exercises in priggishness. When you get there—and I wish you luck, for I thought the main beam of the last wooden bridge was collapsing behind us—drink in the peace in the air, the trees, the riverside village, and forget your San Juan mortgage.

20. The Road to Puerto Plata
(August 11, 1971)

Although published first, this column was written after the previous one. Obviously my trip to Santo Domingo was also a visit to the lost Puerto Rican past.

The road from Santiago to Puerto Plata is in such bad shape that you may be tempted to turn around and return to the ease of Santo Domingo. You would miss one of the most charming corners of the Dominican Republic. It is fitting that the car should go slowly, among the potholes and the boulders that bedevil the road. It is no place to travel 40 miles an hour, seeing nothing, understanding nothing.

From Río Arriba to Yasica it is coffee country. Dominicans from coffee highlands seem different from their compatriots on the vast sugar lands of the plains. They are more independent economically because they have small plots of land on which they raise chickens and plant vegetables and fruits. They don't live bunched together on an acre of shacks, like the cane cutters on the eastern plain, but rather they are scattered all over the mountains, each *bohio* a proud castle. They are active year-round, unlike the cane cutters, who go hungry in the "dead time" between harvests. Electricity hasn't reached many of them, so after 7 o'clock at night the dark stretch between Yasica and Juan de Nina is pierced by candlelight around which families and neighbors huddle. One wonders about the stories they tell within the magic circle of a lantern's light.

Wind and rain and that which makes coffee shrubs bloom and chickens fatten, birth and fear and love and pain-staunching death, these are the constants of mountain life. All the more appreciated because it has been heard before, richer in its repeated telling, the unhurried story saunters along. Children sit on the steps, teasing each other and interrupting the narrator with wide-eyed questions. The well-oiled plot progresses on the grooves of neighbors' laughter and approval, but the traveler drives on, unable to enter the intimate circle of lantern light, a prisoner of his car and of the world that assembled it.

The city traveler is an anonymous outcast in the mountain darkness. But for this exclusion from the circle of light he shall reap his revenge. He will pave the road, making it a hazard for the children and the livestock; he will bring in light bulbs and loud radios and cement boxes which will shut people away from each other; he will buy land but not plant it, and build a weekend villa to entertain scotch drinkers and hire someone to weed the driveway. He will be seeking the peace of the mountain, but it is not for him, neither in the Dominican Republic nor in Puerto Rico.

For whether it be to the mountains around Lake Carite or to those on the road to Puerto Plata, there is no returning from the city jungle, much less when the land is bought like frozen meat and not courted like a princess. There is no access road to simplicity. Our Puerto Rican artists and writers shortchange us when they evoke the lost world of the *jíbaros,* for we are not told how to cope with the pressures of our lives, with the traffic jams, the mortgage payments, and the credit card debts. They tell us to escape into the past and return to the land, but the land won't have us back.

21. The Birth of *Guimica*
(October 16, 1971)

Governor Luis Ferré (1968-1972), an engineer, accomplished pianist, and avid art collector, infuriated the cultural establishment by using offhandedly the word gimmick *at a public occasion. I was still in New York, and I felt I could poke a little fun at all the parties concerned with some etymology.*

When you are out of Puerto Rico you tend to lose contact with the daily give-and-take of politics, and so you find it all the more startling when you read a stray San Juan newspaper. In a recent issue, for instance, I found out that there had been certain pointed exchanges over the word *gimmick*, which Governor Ferré had used in describing incentives to attract mainland industries. It appears that objections to its use arose not only on account of his preference for an American idiom when Spanish equivalents were available but also because of the dubious connotations of the word itself.

Such a serious issue, of course, did not fail to stir my concern, and as soon as I could I went to a reference library and consulted several dictionaries. In Webster's Third International, the first meaning of *gimmick* was "a mechanical device by which a gambling apparatus (as a roulette wheel) can be secretly and dishonestly controlled." It must be quite a gimmick that makes the Puerto Rican economy go, but then there are Casiano and casino in the same hotel. But before people start rushing letters to the beleaguered editor, let us add Webster's second definition, "a new and ingenious device, scheme or idea for solving the problem or achieving an end, a new angle of approach."

This secondary and more respectable meaning of *gimmick* is quite recent. According to Mitford Mathews, the word is defined in a sports magazine of 1928 as "the brake, tip-up, or other device used on games

63

of chance to make them crooked or unfair" to the player. Apparently the word gained currency in advertising circles by the 1940's, when Sir William Craigie defined it as a "stratagem employed to promote a project." Again according to Mathews, in March 1949, *The Chicago Daily News* reported "that the gimmick the White House advisers are most fearful of is the amendment tacked on in the House." By the 1950's Hollywood had latched onto the word, and the question "What's the gimmick?" became standard screenwriters' fare.

Where does the word come from? Most authorities confessed ignorance, but Eric Partridge, in his book *Origins*, suggests it comes from the word *gimbals*, "a contrivance for permitting a body to incline freely," or perhaps from *gimcrack*, "a fanciful scheme, a contrivance, a showy ornament." As such, the word was probably coined in circus and magician circles in the U.S.

Gimcrack itself, however, goes back to the 14th century, where the *Oxford English Dictionary* finds it posing for "some kind of inlaid work in wood." Later it was successively used to denote "a slight or flimsy ornament," "a trumpery article," and "a fanciful notion." *Gimbals*, on the other hand, comes from the medieval French word for twins, which in turn descended from the Latin word for twins (the Gemini of the zodiac) and ultimately from *gemo*, the Greek word for "to be full."

The word *gimmick*, the issue of a long and distinguished line of ancestors going all the way back to Homeric Greece, was born in the U.S. amidst the excitement of magicians' tricks. Since its first modest surroundings, it has been steadily climbing up socially, from slang describing trickery to an advertisers' Americanism to the solid comfort of a berth in Webster's Third International.

Now its social climbing seems to be over, for it has been graced not only by the Governor of Puerto Rico's use but also by the attention of his political opponents. From that to *guimica* is only a step.

Some day, perhaps a century from now, the Real Academia de la Lengua, bowing once more to the pressures of the times, will include *guimica* in its dictionary, and some bald and bleary-eyed academician, preferably in a two-hour conference, will trace to our shores its birth, growth, and ennoblement.

22. Parable of the Good *Pon*
(November 2, 1971)

A pon *is a lift or a ride, and for the many years I didn't drive I was constantly getting* pones, *not only from family and friends, but also from perfect strangers. I gather that nowadays it is harder to get rides in Puerto Rico.*

I was happy to get a needed *pon* the other day from College Park to Santurce. It brought back to mind my friend Cayetano's Parable of the Good Pon.

"There was once an old lady waiting for a *público* on the road from San Germán to Mayaguez. She had left her umbrella home and it started raining the way it rains on the west coast.

"There passed a priest in a borrowed Lincoln Continental; he was a learned man who could speak three dead languages and write in cuneiform. He was on his way to a well-deserved rest, and although he carried fishing gear in the trunk, his mind was so busy with the Book of Prophet Amos that he didn't see the old lady in the rain.

"Then there passed a politician in a blue Cadillac, a well-liked man, even by his opponents, a polite lawyer who gave the correct tip in restaurants. He was on his way to speak at a civic club's monthly dinner, and his topic was Inequities in the Public Works. "Take for instance that old lady in the rain," he said to himself. "Back in San Juan there are many sheltered bus stops and it doesn't rain half as often as on the west coast. Are they getting a fair share of tax revenues used in public works in this area? That should spark a good discussion and I can mention what I did in my district." He drove on trying to polish the example and almost ran into a trailer.

"Then there passed a hippie, one of those the police had driven out of Boquerón with little regard for the niceties of the law. He was driving a Frankenstein of a car, something sired by Studebaker and patched with choice cuts from the carcass of an Edsel. He smoked pot when there was any and shaved almost as often. He saw the old lady in the rain and came to a screeching halt. 'How about a pon?' The old lady climbed in and rode on the clattering relic all the way to Mayaguez.

"Now whom do you think helped the old lady most?" asked Cayetano.

"Indubitably the hippie," I answered.

"You tell that to people. They'll ask you who was the priest and to which party did the politician belong; they'll ask you how thick was the rain and whether the old lady listened to the Weather Bureau bulletins; they'll ask you when did it happen and whether the hippie worked for a living. But they won't see the point."

"Well, I have one question, Cayetano. How did you find out about the story?"

"I was waiting for a bus or a *publico*, too. Would you believe that not even the good hippie offered me a *pon*?"

23. Letter to Doña Alvilda
(December 4, 1971)

Around this time my grandmother, Alvilda Sureda, began to show signs of age.

They tell me, doña Alvilda, that you have been at it again, breaking the ground with a pick to plant some flowers. Of course, neither your 84 years, nor your arthritis, nor the whole town of Cayey can stop you when you decide to have your own way and keep the mount that bears your name blooming. It has ever been so. I should be reproaching you for not following doctor's orders, but instead I find that I'm proud of you.

Born in 1887, the terrible year of the *compontes,* you saw blue-coated American troops entering Utuado in 1898 and the devastation wrought by San Ciriaco Hurricane in 1899. You have been at Las Planadas 60 years, and there you have received and dealt with an incredible array of people—from Muñoz Marín to itinerant evangelical preachers, from South American bishops to Asiatic vegetarians, from university presidents to runaway lunatics, from prospective in-laws to great-great-grandchildren.

There were your old friends coming to visit you in the last *calesas* (carriage coaches) to tell you the latest stories, who was marrying whom in Utuado, and who had gone back to Mallorca. There was the corrupt politician in the thirties who gave you a wad of money to have workers vote for his party and you gave the workers the money and told them to vote for whomever they pleased. There were the soldiers stationed on a nearby hill for whom you made World War II a matter of eating homemade cookies and drinking lemonade behind their officers' back. There were the workers whose machete wounds and sudden ailments you would treat with whatever your medicine cabinet had at the moment—they remembered you afterwards, sending you gladioli bulbs and vegetable seeds from New York, Philadelphia, and Chicago.

And there were the children, wave upon wave breaking upon your rock, arriving with owls, fresh water crabs and shrimp, rabbits, hamsters, hawks, ponies, turtles, puppies, fighting cocks, grasshoppers, tadpoles, and mockingbirds; with bows and arrows, butterfly nets, baseballs, marbles, tops, kites, rockets, chemistry sets, camping tents, and bugles; with incredible appetites and outrageous summer projects to be filed for celebration in your memory.

You have been a strong woman throughout. When the *neblina* (the Cayey mist) in December bundles up the valley for the night and no lights dim the stars except the lightbulb on your porch, there comes over you the manner of the lady of the mountain. The world is at your feet. But then you sigh—you must plant the lower garden again with daisies, like in the old days, and ask somebody what is the matter with the geraniums, and you wonder when to transplant the new batch of petunias. "Tomorrow," you say, "if it doesn't rain, I'll go down after lunch with the pick."

Part IV

Home and the Hues of Nostalgia

24. Doña Juana's Wise Man
(January 3, 1972)

"Tell us again," the children would demand, "the story of the fourth wise man."

Doña Juana would protest that she had already told the story the previous week, but when the chorus of young voices had insisted enough she would wet her lips and start.

"Everybody knows about the three magi who came from the East to find the child Jesus and give him gold, myrrh and frankincense. Well, there was a fourth one who also saw the star in the East."

"What happened to him?"

"Did he get lost?"

"Was his camel no good?"

"Did Herod catch him?"

"I know what happened to him, I remember," the brightest girl would shout. But the others pulled her down. "Let doña Juana tell the story. She knows it best."

"Nicanor had broad shoulders and rode a camel that was as black as the *azabache*. He was bringing the Child a pearl—the roundest, whitest, biggest pearl man ever saw. He was following the star through the *País de las Avellanas*, and he was very close to the spot where he had agreed to meet the other three. That night he stayed at a charcoal burner's *bohío*."

"And the daughter of the house was crying," the brightest girl interrupted.

"Shh! Let doña Juana tell it."

"Yes, the daughter of the house was crying, because they were very poor and her mother was in the municipal hospital, and her father owed money to don Pablo, who owned the woods, and the store, and half the goat they had for milk."

"I know what Nicanor did; do you want me to tell you?" the smart girl would ask the younger children. But they ignored her.

"So good King Nicanor," the old woman said, "asked her what he could do." And the daughter of the house begged him to ride on his black camel two days and two nights to the *País de la Penicilina* and bring back for her mother's cure the blue flower of that country."

"There is no such country," nine-year-old Tomás would protest.

"Perhaps it is Niuyor," said another kid.

"I will ask my teacher."

"So Nicanor rode two days and two nights . . ."

"Without sleeping?"

". . . to the *País de la Penicilina*, and on the edge of the *quebrada* below the tallest mountain he found one fragrant blue flower."

"Did the mother get cured?"

"Yes, they made a tea of the petals. And Nicanor left them all the money he had with him, so that they could get *fiao* at the store again. But when he went to meet the other three magi, they had already left. So he went on to Jerusalem and asked the *alcalde* if he had seen his friends. And the alcalde took him to Pontius Pilate."

"To Herod, to Herod!"

"To Pontius Pilate," doña Juana said firmly, "because he was the *fiscal* that year."

"Why didn't he follow the star?"

"Because the star was in Bethlehem now. So Pontius Pilate told him, 'If you give me that beautiful black camel, I will tell you where your friends went, but if not I will take you to court, and I am the *fiscal*.' Nicanor then gave Pilate the black camel he had had from his father, and Pilate told him to go to Bethlehem."

"And he went on foot?"

"Yes, and it was raining all the way, and the river Jordan had swept away the only bridge. So by the time the fourth wise man got to Bethlehem, the Virgin and Saint Joseph had already taken the Child to Egypt."

"What did Nicanor do?"

"He went to Egypt, but he had nothing to pay for the crossing of the river Danube but the pearl, and he wanted that for the Child. So he worked seven weeks cutting sugar cane. Then he crossed the river Danube and went to each of the 900 *municipios* there, asking if anyone had seen the Child. But nobody had. And he finally gave the pearl to a sick widow whose children had nothing to eat but *malangas.* By now he was lean and had the cough and went barefoot.

"But it wasn't his fault that he didn't get to see the child," protested Tomás.

"Well, *mijo,* he was the wise man of the poor, very unlucky but with a good heart. He didn't get to see Jesus until he was old and unemployed and it was Good Friday. And you know what happened then? He shooed away the flies that were buzzing around the Lord's face. That was better than the gold and the myrrh and the frankincense."

"I don't like the story," the smart girl said, "it's too sad." But twenty years later she was telling it to her children.

25. Remembrances of 1952

(February 19, 1972)

My grandmother was having trouble with her heart, and the predictable family meetings at the hospital sparked this column.

The kids would get a burlap sack from the storeroom on the ground floor and they would enter the coffee grove. They didn't reflect on the chiaroscuro mystery and on the thousand sounds that accompanied their march, for they were kids and they were looking for oranges. In their middle age, having lost the key to childhood, they would think perchance of such moments and say, "Yes, that was what being that age was all about." But it was much more—bantering and bickering, fantasies and illusions, awe and irreverence, all making of such an occasion an expedition. Under the orange trees would bloom a dozen ideas on how to get the most oranges fastest. Would it be best if the oldest climbed and threw them down? But the younger ones knew that inevitably he would pelt them with overripe oranges. And what about shaking the tree? The oldest one had a theory that that would loosen its roots. "Let's pick only those that we can reach without climbing."

"But the best ones are always high up."

And so the hour would pass, and the sack would fill up, even with a grapefruit or two.

"How about picking up *mameyes?*"

"She didn't say she wanted any."

"But she might want to make some marmalade."

"Those plantains look ready," the oldest one would say. "Let's push the *mata* (banana tree) down."

"What if she doesn't want them?"

"If we don't bring them in, they"ll rot."

"Are you sure they are not too thin?"

"They are good for tostones. I know. Come on, let's push."

"Hey, look here, the runaway hens must be sleeping on that tree. We must come tonight and catch them."

"Would she allow us?"

"I'll talk to her," the oldest one said. "But perhaps the two kids can't come."

"We want to come!"

"I don't know," the oldest one said. "It's very serious business. At night a *guaba* might jump on you and bite you."

"There may be ghosts."

"Bandits."

"Do you think there are any Indians still around?"

"My teacher says that there are no Indians left."

"How does she know? They may be hiding."

"All those years?"

"They would have to make fires. You tell by the smoke."

"At night nobody would notice."

"Where would they hide during the day?"

"In the treetops."

"What if somebody cut the tree down?"

"Don't be silly. They would know. They could shoot arrows, perhaps even poisoned darts."

"Hey, it's your turn to carry the sack."

"I carried it a while ago."

"Then it was almost empty."

They made their way back to the house. The grandmother interrupted her ironing to shout: "You're getting your good shirt spoiled carrying those plantains like that."

"It's alright, it's not a good shirt."

"What do you mean it's not a good one? Have you become a millionaire since lunch?"

"The runaway hens! We found their tree. Please, can we go tonight and catch them?"

"We'll see about that. Why did you cut down those plantains? They are still thin."

"We told him, we told him!"

"Please put the sack in the corner. Are you hungry? I baked a cake and there must be some fudge left. We'll make now some orange juice. You, bring glasses for everyone, and the old jar, not the good one they gave me for Mother's Day, and the thing to squeeze the oranges on. And you, wash your hands because you have been playing with the dogs."

"But you'll let us go out tonight with a flashlight, won't you? It's not too far from here . . ."

26. *Publico* Etiquette
(March 31, 1972)

*Three times a week I had to commute to the University of Puerto Rico's
Cayey campus. It was a semester I was teaching at both Río Piedras and
Cayey. I refused to get a driver's license.*

Since the proliferation of cars began, many people have quit taking *publicos*. I suspect many younger people and recent arrivals to the
island have never tried them at all. It may happen that some day, on
account of your sins or out of boredom with your bourgeois life, you
make take one. In that case it would be good if you knew how to do
it properly.

1. *Publicos* are usually taken on the town plazas. Their approach is
signaled by the driver's singsong invitation, "One more, one more for
Humacao." Twenty years ago these calls were more specialized. You
were expected, for instance, to recognize the call, *"Ca-ye-y quen
Cagua'llueve"* ("Direct to Cayey, because in Caguas it rains").

2. You'd show how green you are at the business of taking *publicos*
if you really expected the driver to take off as soon as you got into his
car. The expression "one more" is no less rhetorical than "easy install-
ments" or "jumbo size."

3. The car takes off when the driver eases onto the rear seat one
more passenger than is comfortable for everybody concerned.
Sometimes you are practically sitting on somebody's lap. You should
be grateful that nowadays people are not as likely to be TB cases on
their way to the hospital or proud owners of fighting cocks on the
way to some match.

4. For the first few minutes on the way out there is usually silence,
since the driver is trying to avoid hitting jaywalkers around the plaza,

the town drunkard, the fellow talking with the policeman in the middle of the street, and the orange-seller's cart. Should he hit any of the above, you are expected to take the driver's side in the ensuing argument.

5. After the driver has hit the road, conversation begins, often stimulated by a reckless driver's near miss. The nature of the conversation usually depends on the character of your fellow passengers. Beware of the middle-aged woman with a child who aspires to submit all of you to her monologue. If you spot that trend, it's highly effective to introduce masculine topics like horseracing and spitting contests.

6. If the conversation is general, it's impolite not to take part. You must not declare right away to which political party you belong, because this would deprive you of the opportunity to play the role of arbiter. Every now and then it happens that the driver and all the passengers of a *publico* belong to the same political party. Such happy occasions are marked by competitive efforts to illustrate the ineptitude of the other party.

7. Nowadays children are not as apt to throw up in the course of a trip, but it may not be a bad idea to bring an extra handkerchief.

8. If the driver goes too fast or takes pyrrhic chances in passing on curves, it's standard practice to tell stories about recent accidents and horrible deaths.

9. Sometimes a family sends by *publico* a drunk relative to another branch of the family in another town. Some drunks tell pleasant jokes or sing well; others just breathe on you. Quarrelsome drunks are the driver's responsibility. Fellow passengers usually communicate through eye movements the common attitude to be observed.

10. Tell the driver way ahead of time where you want to get out, lest he cause a major spill by trying to please you instantly.

11. The price of the ride is fixed, unless you're a New York Puerto Rican with a flashy coat and tie, or a fireman returning home from duty late on a holiday night.

27. Nostalgia for Calle Loíza
(April 23, 1972)

The Star's *Sunday magazine was keen on nostalgia, and they asked me for a column. I went back to the Santurce of my memories as a five-year-old.*

When was the last time you really walked in Santurce?

Now, think back. Think back to the days when it was eccentric to live out in *urbanizaciones.* Think back, if you can, to the days of the trolley, when white-suited gentlemen gave their seats to high-heeled ladies on their way to San Juan for their shopping.

Let time roll back, and with time, the car horns, the curly smog over Cataño, anxiety and dissatisfaction with practically everything. Remember the days when Santurce was the hub of the world, before television, when girls had *chaperones,* when priests wore cassocks, when there was an empty lot near the beach where one could play baseball on a lazy Saturday afternoon.

We get off the trolley at the dead end of Ashford Avenue. This is where the Condado ends and the new, hardly paved frontier of Santurce begins. We walk up Krug Street and we are on Calle Loíza, shaded by *flamboyanes,* almonds, and pines and an occasional *Café de la India* tree. There is Calle del Parque, boasting those impeccably painted wooden houses with the wide porches. And on this side of the street we look down sandy King's Court where children walk barefoot on their way to the beach. It's a private street.

Let's cross over—be careful, there might be a car coming: those Fords go fast. Look, there's the Pan American Grocery Store. In December they bring in Christmas trees for the whole parish. And now, down San Jorge Street, to the church, where Padre Rivera is perpetually at work trying to build the Academia. It's a very expensive school; you pay six dollars a month. But the church is the most beautiful in the whole of Santurce, pure neo-Gothic. Padre Rivera, he doesn't want padding on the kneelers or air conditioning, because he says you don't come to church to be comfortable. A good man, but he can sure reprimand young ladies approaching communion in short sleeves.

Now we go back to Loíza by way of Taft Street. Let's take a break under the shade of this tree. See—the spire of San Jorge is the tallest thing around. Listen to the birds. But somebody has the radio on. It's lunch time and Diplo is on in *El Tremendo Hotel*. Santurce worships Diplo and his straight man, the ever-swindled Spaniard, don Tranquilino, who calls despairingly to his late wife, "Come down, Engracia, come down." Remember the time Diplo had don Tranquilino contribute for the "Cuatro de Julio," which turned out to be his friend Julio's guitar?

"*Fuerza! Fuerza de Bayamón!*" An itinerant vendor is selling *modnongo* (tripe) in biscuit cans. The *amoladores* (knife sharpeners), *piragueros*, *revendones, dulceros,* lottery ticket sellers, the man who buys rags, the fellows going by in horse carts selling strings of crabs, they all keep Calle Loíza busy during the day.

Let's continue down Loíza Street. There's Family Court, where Violeta Biascochea has her kindergarten. It's a new thing to have children sing, play, and learn their letters before going on to first grade. Violeta drives around in that huge black car of hers picking up kids everywhere. How can she take all the shouting and jumping and screeching? But the kids learn to read and write before they hit grammar school. Sometimes, when she is busy or sick, her husband Mike takes over, and he always dictates sums: "Now, let's see who's the first one to get this: 12 plus 15 plus 11." "But we have never added anything that big!" "I want to see who's grown-up here." Inevitably the youngest kid, four-year old Aurelio, gets it first.

Behind Violeta's kindergarten is Escuela Goyco, the biggest building on Loíza Street. When a hurricane is announced, people come with food-stuffed sacks to take refuge. On the other side of the street is the Loíza Drug Store, a brand new business opened by a young Barranquitas druggist, don Alfredo, and his wife, doña Lolita, to whom everybody goes when the doctor prescribes penicillin shots. From comic books to sunglasses (which only Americans wear), they sell everything and give counsel to everybody. Not a baby is born on the Calle Loíza whose mother doesn't come in to consult them about diapers, powders, baby food, and teething.

On the corner is Colmado Muñoz. You phone them and they deliver. "Are the kids still down with colds? I hope they get better soon." "Today I need half a pound of *yautía*. Five cents worth of *recao*. One pound of tomatoes, and make sure they're hard because last time there was an overripe one. Do you have any good meat today? Well, send me two-and-a half pounds of that *lomillo*, but wrap it well, because the other day the three chocolate bars got blood over them. Two cans of tomato sauce. Five pounds of rice, the good one, not the other one. Don't take too long, please."

We move down Loíza. On the corner of Carrion Court lives doña Millón, the mother of Luis Laboy, *El Vate's* secretary. She is an invalid and everybody stops by her porch to say hello and trade news. The *tertulia* every night in her living room is an institution. Across the street is the San José movie house where such dramas as *Joan of Arc* with Ingrid Bergman come after they have made the rounds of Ponce de León. Next to it there is the 5 and 10 cents store, but there are some items for which you have to pay 45 cents.

On to Calle Las Flores, where the Loíza Street Post Office hosts one or two lottery ticket sellers and a shoeshine boy, and where the postmaster fills in the money orders for customers. "How do you spell that name?" "I don't know how to spell, but that's just her nickname. You see, she's my aunt's *hija de crianza* (foster child). Everybody calls her by her nickname. Now, her real name . . ."

At Almacenes Infanzón ladies come in with snippets of cloth. "Do you have anything like this? My cousin in Ponce made some curtains with it, and they are beautiful." Out come the bales of cloth and they are spread over the counter. "Now, this isn't exactly like it, but it's nice. Is it very expensive?"

Further on is the Savoy Theater, where with redeemable empty bottles you can get in to see serials. There Calle Loíza really ends, and the Isla Verde Road begins. They are building a new church across Tapia Street, Santa Teresita, for the people in that new development, Ocean Park. Beyond Santa Teresita the coconut groves begin, the picnic beaches, the crab-catchers' huts, the cemeteries. But Calle Loíza, and with it, Santurce, comes to a stop here, on the spot where the Spanish Carmelite, Padre Sanchez, is building a church on a mosquito-plagued *arenal.*

It is the edge of Santurce, 1946. The war has ended and there is hope in the air.

28. On Cantinflas
(Letter from Madrid, August 16, 1972)

I went back to Paris in the summer of 1972 to do additional research in medieval topics. But Madrid was the link-up to Puerto Rico.

There are a number of cheap neighborhood movie houses in Madrid where for the equivalent of a quarter one can see a double feature. To pass in front of a decrepit movie house behind Atocha at 5 in the afternoon, see a Cantinflas movie advertised, and join the throng of children, grandmothers, the unemployed, and the retired is all too easy. How do Spaniards react to Cantinflas?

If that movie house was any indication, Cantinflas goes over big in Spain. The movie was old, and the print every now and then gave trouble, but it was as if it were the newest and freshest film on the market. Cantinflas, in his usual role of maladroit bum, dreams of being D'Artagnan in *The Three Musketeers*. And there he is, riding on a starving horse, stumbling over his sword, launching nonsensical sentences, running into terrible dangers from which his own Mexican ingenuity saves him, and the crowd is roaring with approval. An old Andalusian behind me keeps slapping his knee and saying to himself, "He's too much, that *desgraciao*.?

When Cantinflas-D'Artagnan attempts courtly conversation with Richelieu or the Queen, the crowd is beside itself. The way he handles the formal second plural, the *vosotros*, which is customary in Spain but sounds pompous in Latin America, is magnificent. He keeps getting it mixed up and adding the verb endings to the adjectives. Kids repeat aloud the crazy words he makes up along the way. When Cantinflas appears at the court ball at the end, they applaud.

How little have Cantinflas' movies aged. They are basically atemporal, and they seem as appealing in this corner of the Spanish-speaking world as in Mexico or in Puerto Rico itself. It's easy for all to identify with Cantinflas, and perhaps the poorer the audience is, or the more innocent, the more spontaneous the reaction. You have to have been intimidated by authorities or pushed around by bullies to savor fully Cantinflas' outwitting of them. Of course, the powers that be suffer only a momentary discomfiting. Cantinflas wins only skirmishes; he wakes up no longer D'Artagnan, but just the bum off the street who has wandered into a studio. There will be other movies which will show him again in jail or out of a job or dreaming up some impossible enterprise.

Some 15 to 20 years ago, when Cantinflas was the rage in Puerto Rico, there was a certain snobbishness that found him "vulgar." He lacked respect and was suspected of teaching children, servant girls, and grocery store messengers to be pert. His movies were not shown in the best movie houses of the day, which were reserved for the latest technicolor films out of Hollywood. Then Cantinflas appeared in *Around the World in Eighty Days* and gained respectability. He couldn't be that subversive if he appeared in an American movie. It became alright to see *El Padrecito* or *El Bombero Atómico*.

Yet seeing Cantinflas in Madrid, where life resembles so much that of Santurce 20 years ago, one cannot help sensing that the establishment was right in feeling threatened by Cantinflas. His wit is egalitarian. He has shown all along that if a bum can be ridiculous on account of his ignorant speech and his patched up trousers, an aristocrat or an official is even more vulnerable to ridicule through his efforts to maintain the distances and the privileges of rank.

In Cantinflas' movies the police chiefs, the rich ladies with their French poodles, the bossy men behind mahogany desks are destined to be found out, not as corrupt or vain or cowardly, but as human as Cantinflas himself. Behind the cigar or the insignia of rank is somebody who can respond to the same human drives as Cantinflas, undermining the hierarchy of blood, rank, and wealth. All are equally worth the same *consideración*, because all are like Cantinflas, and to push him or to deceive him is to doom oneself to an equal fate.

29. Utuado in 1900
(August 26, 1972)

In the last two years of her life, my grandmother managed to intrigue me with the history of her native municipality, Utuado. I wound up doing something much different from what she would have expected, but at least this first column was in synch with her view of the past.

Doña Alvilda is in the hospital, which can be a bewildering experience when one is 85. She draws strength for the ordeal from her memories, which reach back to the *tiempos de España* (Spanish days) and the days when Utuado was adjusting to the new American regime.

It's an attractive, staid Utuado that emerges from her recollections. Everybody knew everybody else, "and if somebody in the family died everybody mourned, and if somebody was born everybody celebrated."

She likes to remember the plaza. "When I was a girl, the other girls and myself would congregate around a bench in the plaza. We would be breaking out in laughter so often that people would take detours not to walk past us. They were afraid we would laugh."

The church was the center of life. "When the feasts of Our Lady would come, the Hijas de María would decorate her altar. They were great afternoons. I was the one who would climb up to put the velvet cloth behind the statue, for the others were afraid of falling. There was an older, single man who would come to help us, and we kept sending him on errands. We badgered him so much."

On Sunday afternoons families would go out in the *calesas* (horse drawn carriages) to visit each other and have *meriendas* (snacks). It was always important for a young girl to see in which direction the family would drive, for on such occasions she might get a glimpse of her boyfriend, and then secret signals would be exchanged. In time he would begin to make formal visits to the family.

I ask her about the invasion. "Those were hard times for everybody." She remembers the day the blue-coated soldiers marched into town. There was a garrison, and the officers tried to get to know the people by visiting them after dinner for the *tertulia.*

"Somebody suggested to my father that he leave the gate open downstairs, so that the officers would know that they were welcome. That night instead of officers some soldiers came in. My sister was playing the piano. Then one of the soldiers put his feet on the coffee table. My father never opened the downstairs gate again at night. They may have been drunk, those soldiers. The table is still in the family."

The San Ciriaco Day Hurricane (August 8, 1899) even more than the invasion unsettled life in Utuado. One of her sisters, Margarita, died of tetanus fever that same month. Many planters were ruined, and some sold out and left for Mallorca and Barcelona, "and so many friends were separated and never saw each other again."

"Utuado was so far from everything then. It took almost six hours to get to Arecibo in a *calesa.* After I got married we would go to the theater in Arecibo, not only us, but several couples we knew. We would all leave together, each couple in their *calesa.* It was a beautiful road, but too long. We would be back from Arecibo at midnight, or one in the morning, very tired. But it was such fun, all the couples on the road, going to the theater in Arecibo."

30. The Art of Lottery Tickets

(January 2, 1973)

It's sometimes a matter of concern to see young professional men and women carelessly buying lottery tickets. Of course, it all comes from their having studied in the States, where, among other things, they may have absorbed the idea that one lottery ticket is statistically just as good as any other. In this regard, as in many others, the recently returned professional must be reeducated upon reentry.

The following rules may be of help to those earnest young people who up to now have been committing one faux pas after the other in this sensitive area.

1. Just as you don't buy any bottle of wine you may see on supermarket racks, you don't take the first lottery ticket a seller may offer. He or she may be trying to get rid of an ugly number, or a number that is handicapped by an ill-wisher's evil eye, or one that has already got the first prize 37 months ago. If it's a ticket for the *extraordinaria*, these factors would make a seller desperate enough not to allow you to buy the number you want without also taking at least one ticket from this ugly number.

2. As every man, woman, and child the length of this island knows, it is important to look at the last digit. Numbers ending in 4 or 8, for instance, aren't as lucky as numbers ending in 7, 3, or 2. If the previous week the winner ended in 5, a ticket ending in 1 or 9 may be a wise buy.

3. BUT the ending is not the whole story. You must add them up. The number 41851 may look like an ugly number, but it adds up to 19, which is St. Joseph's day, and that's lucky. Other numbers may add up to 13 (St. Anthony's) or your birthday, or the new governor's age (19999). Those are good buys.

4. It's also important to know who else has bought the same number. Here the lottery ticket seller may be willing to say that the mother superior of the nuns'convent or a mother of 14 children has bought a dollar's worth, but he or she may hide from you the fact that a cross-eyed drunk also bought a share. Beware.

5. If you buy a lot of the same number, let's say $10 worth, it's lucky to give a couple of tickets to a friend in need or to your barber as a tip. This act improves a number's chances, as everybody knows.

6. Where do you put the tickets after you buy them? Men usually put them in their wallets and women on top of their dressers, but some people have special locations of their own—under holy statues, next to pictures of beloved people, inside a shoe, and so on. It's important not to shift them! A ticket may be warming up for first prize, but frequent handling may impair its chances.

7. Before the drawing, don't refer aloud to your ticket; at least, don't name all the digits. You can say, for instance, "I have bought a 14,000" or "I have bought something that adds up to my age," but it's extremely foolhardy to say, "I have bought $3 worth of 36363." Of course, if you buy the same number week after week it's another story, for everybody knows that it is your number and half your clan will have checked it on the lottery list before you yourself do. But the rules for buying the same ticket are different, since the numbers come in dreams and flashes and after 22 years win you first prize.

8. How do you check the lottery list? At times it's painful to see some young, impatient person give a glance at the paper and rip up some tickets. Again, it's like wine. You don't empty a cup in one gulp. You savor it, going down the list slowly.

31. A Sense of "Place"
(April 17, 1973)

A year ago a fellow armed with a piece of lead pipe interrupted my class on the Cayey college campus.

"Is there anyone here from Cidra? I want to hit somebody from Cidra on the head." I assured him that there was no one from Cidra in the class. The anti-*Cidreño* headhunter departed, and no one knows whether he eventually found a victim or entered an asylum. Of course, what was considered strange about him was not that he was looking for a *Cidreño* to hit, but that he was doing so off a baseball field or outside the town plaza during the Patron Saint feast, when the hereditary Cayey-Cidra rivalry usually claims its toll in broken heads.

People in the metropolitan area naturally deplore such things and prefer hating people they have seen only in the newspapers—Communists, the Mafia, and foreign intellectuals. But people in the metropolitan area, especially those who live in *urbanizaciones* (subdivisions), tend to lose their sense of "place" and "myth." For, as the Trinidadian writer V. S. Naipaul says, a place, to be fully a "place," has to have a story attached to it. The more fantastic the story, the more powerful the name of the place becomes. A name becomes mythical, has properties attached to its very mention, confers distinction or shame.

And so in Puerto Rico, Arecibo is the "Villa del Capitán Correa," and this title makes all *Arecibeños,* by definition, daring. People from Yauco are supposed to be exclusive, people from Fajardo barefaced (*Cariduros*), people from Quebradillas pirates, and those from Isabela (cocks) untowardly aggressive. In island lore, Guayama is addicted to witchcraft and Cabo Rojo to smuggling, while Arroyo is full of non-Spanish Europeans and San Germán is home to the "truly old families." And, of course, even if Sanjuaneros themselves have forgotten it, the rest of the island knows that the *gente de la losa* are boastful and overbearing.

There are stories to back these reputations, and no town sees itself the way its neighbors do. There are, if you want, two sets of myths, one circulating locally and the other peripherally, but each set has served to situate an individual outside his den. He is always expected to catch compliments or allusions. Thus when somebody from Cayey says, "So you are from La Cidra . . ." he is supposed to be scoring with this allusion to the time when Cidra was just a barrio of Cayey.

The trouble with the metropolitan area is that there are not enough myths in circulation. It has grown too fast, and the names of the *urbanizaciones* evoke little more than real estate values. There is no story about someone from Bayamon Gardens who has cruised the Caribbean with a crew of pirates and given half his share to the poor. There are no stories of miraculous pictures disappearing from churches only to turn up in trees in Hillside or Parkville. The name "Levittown" doesn't trigger a memory of a desperate romance between an Indian girl and a Spanish hildalgo, and Apollo hasn't turned anyone into a tree in Alto Apolo. Maybe a hundred years from now there will be a legend of buried treasure in Laguna Gardens or a byword about the generosity of people from Venus Gardens, but right now they remain indistinct.

Developers have tried to "create places" by giving them fancy names, but the names sound hollow. Witness, however, the way people in Lajas received their famous son, with a banner saying, "Lajas— Ciudad Cardenalicia" (Lajas, the Cardinal's City), or how Carolina has begun to harvest its Roberto Clemente fame. Maybe that's what the Pentagon has never understood about Culebra and Vieques—that they are not just convenient locations for firing ranges, but that they are "places," and that all Puerto Ricans, since childhood, have fantasized about these storied islands off the Island which can be visited for the price of a cold beer. Maybe most people never take the trip, but that has made the fantasy all the more powerful.

32. Professor McDowell
(April 28, 1973)

It was a standard family joke that my mother had to see the Weather Bulletin every night. More than Professor McDowell (a faculty colleague in Río Piedras who I would occasionally see at the campus post office), it was my mother I wanted to needle with this column. I didn't make a dent in her routine.

It wasn't long after television started in San Juan that Professor McDowell began forecasting the weather on the new medium. At first it was at 6:15 in the evening, and then it was placed after the evening news, and there he is, faithfully, every night, a living link to half of Sanjuaneros' childhood. In fact, a whole generation has been born, grown up, and gone to the University of Puerto Rico with Professor McDowell's weather, so that it is perfectly impossible to imagine hurricane warnings, the rainfall at Dos Bocas, and the forecast for San Juan, Ponce, and Mayaguez without seeing on the top right corner of the picture, like the regal image in a British postage stamp, the professor's paternal profile.

McDowell has replaced *Juracán*, the Indian storm god, and those crusty wielders of divine punishment, San Ciriaco, San Felipe, and San Ciprián, as the giver and taker of good and bad weather. He has given us only one hurricane, Santa Clara, but everyone knows that he tried hard to avert it, and although he failed in 1956, he succeeded in far chancier years. He has given us more good weather than bad, but, of course, southern cattlemen still have a grudge against him for the long drought of the mid-1960's, and there were two bad years of flash floods which northern lowlanders would have wanted him to wish away, the way he does with hurricanes. But on the whole McDowell

91

has given the tourists plenty of sun and the metropolitan area plenty of cool night breezes. When we need rain, he hops about until he gets it, and when there is too much of it he obtains relief.

As a ritual figure McDowell commands respect and obedience. I know people who have become compulsive about turning on his report every night and won't water plants, open windows, go to the movies, or take a trip to Cayey without consulting him. But the knowledge of possessing such authority hasn't gone to McDowell's head. Others would have devised novel kinds of weather, promising snow or tornadoes or tidal waves; they would have got high and mighty with hail and frost; they would have thought up apocalyptic events or would have changed the times of tides to suit popular demand. Not Professor McDowell. To my knowledge the only time he has entertained any fancy was last summer, when it seems he tried to garner for San Juan the island-wide record for heat, held since the beginning of the century by San Lorenzo. But Sanjuaneros didn't think much of the attempt, so he gave up. It was a wise move, because the streets were starting to melt.

On and off there has been a question whether McDowell plays favorites in assigning weather to different towns. For instance, it is alleged that in February or so every year he satisfies Adjuntas by allowing it to have very cold temperatures. The ones who complain, of course, are people from Aibonito, who get red with rage when any place besides itself manages to score lower temperatures. Others point out that Caguas is seldom allowed to have a weather of its own, although it's bigger than Aguadilla. Maybe it's just the way he mentions Aguadilla's temperature that gives the impression of favoritism, for the name admittedly is long and has the attractive double "l" to tarry with.

In time of drought some of McDowell's fans worry. It used to be the custom in Trujillo Alto and Ciales when it didn't rain to have processions to the river with a saint's statue. If after several processions rain wasn't forthcoming, the saint's statue would get a dunking. Knowing how impetuous those Corsicans on the south coast are, one is glad to know that the drought there is ending. It would be lèse-majesté to have our weatherman dunked.

Part V

A Time for Dissent

33. Revolt of the Trees
(August 31, 1973)

Then the day came when the remaining trees in the metropolitan area of San Juan formed a union. Out of sentiment (because somebody said that it was probably the last of its species within the city limits), they elected president the *ceiba* on Chardon Street, near the Tres Monjitas Industrial Park. The secretary was a mutilated mahogany from De Diego Avenue in Santurce, and a *laurel de la India* collected union dues.

They met on alternate Wednesday nights on a Cantera parking lot, and one time they decided to have a march, except they didn't know where to march to. So the almond tree from in front of the First National in Hato Rey waved its branches, and although he tended to be wordy they let him talk. "Mr. President," he said, "and dear surviving colleagues. We have before us the most pressing question of our unionized existence. We must make a gesture. It's imperative that we make a bold gesture or the present disastrous course of affairs will climax in our utter ruin."

"Hear, hear," said a frisky *flamboyán* from one of the *urbanizaciones,* but the *ceiba* frowned.

"A march," said the almond tree, "a parade, promenade, or procession would serve to air our grievances before that public that is ever captivated by novelty but seldom committed to positive action. And we want positive action!"

A sleepy mango in the back, thinking that the almond had finished, applauded, but the latter went on.

"Therefore I think that marches don't suffice. We have signed petitions. We have issued press releases. Our worthy president has been interviewed for a TV show. But none of these things have aroused the

95

proper reaction, and we remain an exploited, threatened class. How many trees are left on Loíza Street? Where are our brothers from Calle del Parque, McLeary, King's Court, Ashford Avenue, Magdalena? Daily some of our brothers are ripped out of the ground. The telephone company lops off our limbs. The electric company believes that the only good tree is an axed tree. Everywhere they let us die of neglect. Who can guarantee that in 20 years we shall still stand on Plaza de Armas or at the Julia Clinic, the University, or Ocean Park? I propose, therefore, that we do something bold. Let us occupy a public building and refuse to come out until 10,000 trees are planted on the city's sidewalks and on government—owned land."

The opinion of the assembly was divided, some holding, with an old backyard *grosella* tree, that only a boycott be contemplated ("but a boycott of what?" demanded a *liligayo*), and others backing the proposed building seizure. All throughout, the *ceiba* kept its peace, trying to avoid, if possible, a conflict of generations that would imperil its leadership, but since no solution seemed forthcoming and leaves were starting to fall, it finally intervened.

"This building seizure scheme of yours," the *ceiba* said, addressing the almond, "will end up alienating public support. We would never be able to choose the right building to seize, and you never know whom they might send in to evict us. The boycott, on the other hand, doesn't seem realistic, considering how few we are. I still think that we should march, but not on the Capitol or any other place, but away from San Juan. Let's all go to El Yunque for a week. That way we'll be able to enjoy some vintage humus at the same time that we make a point."

The following morning there was a mammoth traffic jam on 65th Infantry Avenue. The trees were leaving the city. Ahead of the column went the gaunt *ceiba*, carrying the presidential gavel. Then came the others in order of age, pines, laurels, mangos, and bucayos, and the palm trees kept everybody in order and had Band—Aids for sore roots. At the rear came 10 *robles* distributing leaflets, and it was said that they were humming the "Internationale."

"The trees abandon the city," the papers announced the next morning, and for two days people cared, and on the third they filled in the holes with cement.

34. The Value of Dissent
(November 28, 1973)

There was a great deal of harassment of Puerto Rican dissenters in the early 1970's, fed by the right's fears and the center's indecision.

Recently a columnist in *El Mundo* suggested that all pro—independence people in important government posts should be forced to resign. The idea was that these people were all too dangerous to be trusted in responsible positions. The curious thing was that this was the same columnist who not too long ago was protesting that the pro—statehood government of Luis Ferré was attempting to purge commonwealth supporters from the government and from the press.

Even more curious, however, was the lack of public reaction to this McCarthyist proposal. If anything, the idea seemed to be gaining acceptance. Another columnist in the same paper was warning the public that communists were taking over the Cayey campus of the University of Puerto Rico. In private and in public people were saying that the Governor should "clean up" the University of "extremist elements." The inheritance of bishop Manso, who brought the Spanish Inquisition to our shores in the 16th century, seems to be weighing heavily on us.

The truth is that we loudly proclaim belief in democracy, freedom of expression, and a free press on the one hand, but on the other we discourage, revile, and suppress dissent. It is dangerous to disagree in Puerto Rico. The offices of a party and its organ, *Claridad,* are repeatedly the target of bomb attacks. A professor, Arturo Meléndez, is nominated by Dr. Cobas to fulfill secretarial functions in a university body, and several months later another *El Mundo* columnist uses this nomination as an instance of Dr. Cobas's attempt to introduce "subversive individuals" into the university's top echelons. Professor José Arsenio Torres expresses in public convictions that are controversial, to be sure, but consistent with the tenor of his past interventions in university life, and he is physically assaulted in a university building. People oppose the Vietnam War, the blockade on Cuba, or the super—port, and they become the objects of persecution and violence.

Do we believe in democracy? Then let's learn to value dissent. It makes the decision—making process slower, to be sure, but the decisions that result from this process have more lasting value, since all possible elements have to be taken into account. Dictatorships are more efficient than democracies, but they make more costly errors. They make the trains run on time, but they choose the destinations of passengers who ride on those trains.

History has shown us who, in the long run, did more good for his people, Trujillo or Muñoz Marín. There was no crime on the streets of Ciudad Trujillo because there was only one criminal and he was locked up in the presidential palace most of the time. There was no trash on the streets in Ciudad Trujillo because there was hardly anything people could afford to part with. There was order in Ciudad Trujillo because laws were made easily to cope with all situations.

But democracies take a lesser risk. They allow the criminal to be free so long as his innocence is not disproved, but they don't allow the dictator to rule if his guilt is proven. Democracies allow the demagogue to speak out because the demagogue may be an eight—year—old shouting that the president strutting down the street without any clothes on is naked. They allow dissent because the possibility of disagreement is part and parcel of the sharing of responsibility, and this sharing is the nemesis of tyranny.

35. *El Nacimiento*
(December 8, 1973)

Germans call it a putz, *Spaniards a* belén, *others a Christmas* crèche.
But with us it was always El Nacimiento.

When we were kids, it was about this time of the year when we
started asking: "When are we going to buy the Christmas tree? When
are we going to lay out the *nacimiento?*" Invariably the answer was:
"It's too early, December is just starting."

But it was never too early to start planning the *nacimiento,* the
miniature Bethlehem with the nativity scene. Ours was an imperialis-
tic Bethlehem; it kept growing year after year until one Christmas it
took up almost a whole room.

It was a complicated affair which required a wholesale family
effort. Brown paper had to be splotched with green, and those were
the days before spray cans, so that a crisis was sure to impend on
whether the back porch would be stained or not. There were all kinds
of tin cans with plants growing in them, so that there could be trees
in Bethlehem. And then, of course, there was always this grave matter: are we going to have a river this year, a real river? One year we
finally had one with cement and tin foil paper, and after that time, the
river, like everything else in that mythical Bethlehem, kept growing in
size and splendor.

The *nacimiento* had Japanese cardboard houses with snow—
capped roofs. There was a red, blue, and yellow windmill. There was
a crenellated medieval castle, Herod's residence, and it loomed men-
acingly in the distance. It was garrisoned by crusaders and a couple
of camel—riding bedouins.

The rest of Bethlehem's personnel, if less martial, was just as exotic: blue—coated shepherds standing in Prussian attention, Mexican peasants, a donkey—riding black—hatted personage (dubbed *El Gallego*; his hat, according to the carol, was doomed to be eaten by the ox in the stable), a plastic giraffe, a fellow playing the accordion, and an attaché case—carrying bureaucrat.

Everybody was always en route to the manger. The Magi always started out from the farthest point but they kept creeping closer day by day with their retinue of camels and attendants. By Three Kings' Day, everybody had got to the manger: shepherds, sheep, chickens, cows, fishermen, woodsmen, the attaché case bureaucrat, and even a bedouin or two. Of course, esthetically motivated sisters didn't approve of such crowding, but with the connivance of older brothers, one was always able to get everybody there in a couple of forced marches.

I still can't imagine Christmas any other way. After having to wade through all kinds of footnote—ridden articles on Palestinian geography and tetrarchs and inter—testamental literature and the Dead Sea Scrolls and Lucan theology and the Lord knows what else, the word "Bethlehem" automatically brings to mind the cast and the scenario of the *nacimiento*—the shepherd playing his flute to his mongrel dogs, the old man pointing out the way to Santos and Félix, the pre—war woolen German sheep, the sturdy camels, the cardboard Japanese houses, and the giraffe peering from behind the stable.

It is as if all these had a platonic existence; as if some day one was supposed to meet them all and politely inquire how the accommodations were at the inn, what it was like to ride on a camel; as if one would get the chance to intercede with the innkeeper, so that they wouldn't eat the fat woolly ram in the pen or chase away the plastic giraffe.

36. De Moca

(December 29, 1973)

There is a TV ad that makes one brood. It promotes an amusement park that has much to offer, so much in fact, that it makes a kid worry that his dad will forget about the schedule for the bus home. "And where are you from?" the benign interviewer asks. "From Moca." "*De Moca!*" the interviewer echoes in patronizing admiration.

The ad is charming, and the intention behind the Moca theme, no doubt, is to emphasize the all—island appeal of the park. But there is also the unintentional effect of making one think of Moca itself, which, according to a recent press release, is one of the five towns where the pilot food stamp program will be implemented. For Moca is one of those forgotten municipalities where no news is supposed to develop, but where the retelling of the Puerto Rican success story is beginning to jar the ears.

In 1968 Moca broke its generation—long attachment to the *Populares* and elected a New Progressive Party administration by a 77—vote margin. It was then one of the poorest municipalities on the island. In 1972 Moca returned to the PDP fold by a margin of some 150 votes, and with a percentage of PDP votes smaller than the combined PDP and People's Party percentages in 1968. The Puerto Rican Independence Party, on the other hand, climbed from 63 votes in 1968 to 422 in 1972 (from 1 to 4 percent of the total vote), a proportion that is still below that party's island—wide average, but that is sufficient to hold the balance of power in Moca.

The town remains to this day among the bottom 10 in per capita income. Obviously the food stamp program, which could help local retailers as well as the unemployed, is not contemplated by anyone as the permanent solution to Moca's problems. Yet with the prospect of fewer factories opening up on the island this coming year, one won-ders how long it will be before towns like Moca will be able to stand on their own feet. Are people there supposed to cling to their dignity and weather the coming economic storm any way they can?

Are they supposed to migrate or sell avocados on the roads or receive free training as electricians and plumbers in the hope that some day there will be enough fixtures in Moca to mend? Or shall the town become an exporter of carpenters to the metropolitan area, workers who leave in *públicos* at 4 a.m. and return at 9 p.m. to watch their kids sleep? How easy it is for Sanjuaneros to contemplate hard times from behind the iron grill bars of their porches.

What can be done to help Moca out? That's the sort of question elected officials are supposed to answer, but they have more pressing commitments. Moca is too small a stake in the political racetrack. Still, on an island where we import cases and frames for eyeglasses, where chain stores sell souvenirs of Puerto Rico made in Japan, where *platanutre* (fried plantain chips) is brought from Florida, Christmas glass ornaments from Eastern Europe, and Christmas crib figures from Spain and Italy, a municipal government, if allowed by law, could open and operate (and perhaps later sell) one or two fac-tories that would help the local situation and the island's balance of payments.

It is easy to point out what is not working and extremely hard to come up with solutions. But parting shots are easier: Wouldn't it be much better for Moca if the municipality ran an amusement park there? Then the well—dressed kid in the ad would be worrying about missing the Bayamón or the Ponce bus.

37. On Mosquito Nets

(Letter from Cayey 1, January 25, 1974)

If the editor's patience lasts, this is the first of ten letters from Cayey. I want to think of this and the nine columns that follow as a unit, as something I would publish as a book if I were the kind of person who had the patience to write and publish books.

And if it were a book, the reader would have next to this, the first page, the drawing of a harried professor handing in his semester's marks at the Registrar's Office in Río Piedras. For there are few things in the world that give you such a sense of freedom as exchanging your graded lists for computer cards that certify that you have completed a semester.

You have given good marks to good students, mediocre marks to students you couldn't talk into doing better, and bad marks to students who couldn't make of you a better teacher. That's perhaps why one is so reluctant to give bad marks. It's an acknowledgment that there is an impasse (pardon the pun).

With the semester over one can indulge again in idealism. One can dream of the perfect course next semester, or of the completion of research on a historical problem so abstruse that there may be only three people in the world who realize it is a problem. Or you can take off to Cayey and sanity, for according to my good friend Father Antonio Quevedo, there is a receding frontier between the world of illusion and the world of sanity, and at present that frontier lies somewhere between Caguas and Cayey. When he has a chance he takes off to Aibonito, but Cayey baptized me, and only the cold air of *El Torito* has the virtue of rescuing me from the world of illusion.

And at present the air is cold indeed. One doesn't last until the evening news. The first night I arrived I was looking at 9 p.m. for a blanket under which to dive. But first I had to set the mosquito net, a matter so serious that *San Juan Star* readers should be warned about it.

According to an unpublicized survey I made, 92 percent of this paper's readers no longer use mosquito nets. They were brought up in the disciplined ritual of putting up a mosquito net every night, but some time in the late 50's or the 60's they abandoned the ways of their fathers and took to window screens. This was a part of their shifting from wooden to concrete houses and from a traditional to a permissive society, so that now their children don't know what it is to put up a mosquito net every night; as a result, an undisciplined generation has grown up.

Impulsive readers are likely to write to the editor saying that, although they haven't done it in years, it is very easy indeed to put up a mosquito net. Of course, they live in a world of illusion, as I did myself before the University Registrar's Office gave me my freedom. There should be an Olympiad for those who haven't hung a mosquito net in 12 years, and I bet none at the first try would break 4 minutes.

Here you are, on top of *El Torito,* shivering from head to foot, disentangling a mosquito net. You must look for hooks, the same ones that were there when you were 10 years old. Three are visible, but a picture was hung from the fourth some 15 years ago, and it takes some dusting of the brain to realize it has a plurality of functions. At the first try you get it all wrong: the string doesn't reach one hook. You decide then to turn it around, but you end up with an upside down net. Patience, let's try once again—but first it must be disentangled.

In the end, after you have put the net at right angles with the bed, you finally get an extra length of string and return to the original arrangement. Then you crawl inside. Careful, or you'll rip one of the strings. Tuck all the corners in. Ah, there you are, lord and master of an enclosed space where no insect can enter. You have triumphed over chaos; you deserve a good night's rest.

38. Bagatelle

(Letter from Cayey 2, January 30, 1974)

On the mountaintop one wakes up in the cold and darkness with a distant trumpeting of cocks' crowing. It's the sort of thing Abelardo Díaz Alfaro has written about—the mist, the morning cup of coffee, the dew drops on the grass. It's the lost world of our traditionalist poets and politicians, and while the mist lasts one is back in the 1940's, wondering about the day's weather, planning what to harvest, what to weed and clear, what to plant.

One must dig in the garden, as Voltaire's Candide discovered after his travels. But the garden has been overrun with weeds and underbrush, and while one hacks away a sense of futility develops. "What's the good of it? In a couple of weeks the weeds will be back." It's surprising how quickly the wrist and the forearm begin to protest against the unaccustomed swing of the machete. And then there are the stubborn weeds one tries to pull out. They give a good fight and suddenly yield, making one lose one's balance. No wonder then that one begins to take longer breaks to wipe sweat from the brow.

At the Bois de Boulogne in Paris, there is a rose garden, Bagatelle. If you go there between June 15 and July 10, you'll see one of the truly great spectacles in the world, thousands and thousands of roses, of all sizes, colors, and kinds, from the latest hybrids to the simplest wild creepers. On a sunny weekday afternoon Bagatelle is a peaceful haven for students, who recline under the pine trees to review their class notes before the exams. The refreshment kiosk is expensive ($1 for a glass of lemonade), but if you are lucky enough to have someone foot the bill you can sit back and see high society ladies exchanging pleasantries while their children and their dogs cavort on the myrtle alleys. Well, it is of Bagatelle one thinks when hacking up the underbrush and weeding out the garden. It is as if the fantasy of recreating Bagatelle speeded up one's arm, although at the end of an hour one has cleared little more than a three-foot-by-three-foot square.

The meager output is no handicap for one's thoughts. One remembers turn-of-the- century photographs of town plazas with all kinds of flowers. Why is it that there is no comparable adult recreational area now? Everybody has retreated to the walled privacy of home gardens and lawns, to the foolishness of planting trees that will be too big for the backyard and of putting in dahlia bulbs which the mice will devour.

Few flowers are planted in public parks and plazas "because people steal them." Besides, people don't walk through parks anymore—these are for kids to ride bicycles in, or for adolescents to smoke what may be marijuana. San Juan people ride in their cars and watch television and go shopping; they go to each other's parties and every now and then catch the rare good movie which the lords of a virtual monopoly of theaters may toss them. And the strange thing is that Sanjuaneros have conformed to these routines. They have lost that sense of earnestness which would keep alive before their eyes alternatives to the rat races they have made of their lives. In San Juan one seldom exercises one's mind or body, and that is why one has to come to Cayey and is swinging an unsharpened machete.

39. A Gathering of Cousins
(Letter from Cayey 3, January 31, 1974)

On Sunday there is a spontaneous rally of cousins, for on this day by chance almost everybody shows up. José thinks of climbing down the mountain, to see our Uncle Jorge who has moved recently. Everybody teams up; most haven't walked down and up the mountain since adolescence and the occasion is too good to miss. We start through the coffee grove down a steep footpath.

Now, where were you, San Lorenzo, on that afternoon when Provita slipped on the muddy trail and fell, once, twice, three times, to the sound of general laughter? In vain did Fitin fashion a goodly walking stick for her; too late did he think of it, for the red badge of mud was imprinted on her back. But Mercedes, avoiding our treacherous tracks, skirted the path, and the *cadillos* (nettles) transformed her into an armadillo. Much would her son Jorge toil to rescue her from her plight, but that is another epic.

After the grove a grassy slope, down which some run spiritedly and some prudently negotiate their footing. And at the uncle's house, *tía* Laura has coffee, fresh orange juice, home made cookies, and coconut pudding. There we are joined by my brother and his family. There are some who would go with them in the car ride back up the mountain, but a challenge develops and bravado takes over. In fact, now even the ones who came by car want to climb on foot.

But it is one thing to climb down a mountain, a simple pastime for cousins on a Sunday afternoon, a mere matter of avoiding pitfalls and not slipping all the way down. It is another to climb up that same mountain, even if it is by that pack mule trail which is the *Cuesta de los Ortegones*. Javier leads the way; he is interested in marking time and soon we lose sight of him. Charito looks for wild green orchids,

José pulls his wife up the slope, but Provita begins to say that this climb has been a great mistake. Two *guaraguaos* (sparrow hawks) hover above us. "There you are," somebody says, "they know and they are waiting." But the *guaraguaos* don't develop an interest in our potential carcasses, and with a single beat of their wings they ride on the wind the whole distance we still have to cover. "Showoffs," we shout at them.

Halfway up Ana Mari and Carmenchu break from the group; no more rests for them, no sir; they are going straight to the top. And they do it, while mere mortals pant and huff, and Mercedes covers all the chinks in her armor with *cadillos*. But José is calculating distances, and I am praising the excellent view.

Provita points to the ravine to our right: "Do we have to cross that?" "We could if we wanted to get there fast, but we are not going to." Whereupon she revives considerably, because she has feared all along that we would have to go down and up the muddy ravine sides. In fact, she begins to plot how to trap absent members of the family into a similar hike. By the time we reach the top, she is actually saying that people ought to do this more often, if only because gasoline is getting scarce.

And I think that all over Puerto Rico there may be thousands of people like us who would get a kick out of climbing a mountain, like they did when they were kids, when there was no TV, fewer cars, and much more laughter.

40. On the Importance of Symbols
(February 6, 1974)

Man has a peculiar capacity to express himself as other. He can attach his identity to a symbol, and that symbol can ride the vicissitudes of life and by doing so fulfill his deepest aspirations. A person can identify himself as king or beggar, as Guelf or Ghibelline, as judge or as fashioner of his own law, and to the degree that others accept his roles he may consider himself a success. He can find in material objects an expression of his loves and hates, so that nations can go to war over the color of a rose, like 15th- century England, or over the insertion of an iota in a creed, like the 5th-century Roman Empire. Man can attach so much importance to symbols that he may die rather than step on a crucifix or turn his back on a flag.

In democracies personal and material symbols achieve recognition through the majority's consensus. One person can call himself governor and ride his limousine through the gates of Fortaleza while another, claiming the same title, may wind up in the madhouse. The only difference between them is that the first is recognized as such even by his opponents, while the second can claim no other recognition than the secret voice within his brain. One person can practice medicine and receive public acclaim, while another can attempt the same and find himself in jail. The only difference may be that the first is licensed to practice and the other is not. One person can wear the badge of the Cross of Malta on his forearm, and he will be honored as a veteran; another may choose to wear a swastika and find himself the object of rejection. The difference in the reaction to symbols may seem arbitrary, but each has a history behind it, and the waters of the Atlantic Ocean would not suffice to cleanse the second from its infamy.

So man makes and records his history through symbols, and the institutions he fashions in compact with others are made manifest to all through symbols—the governor's seal, the diploma on the wall, the regiment's badge. Part of the educational process is to develop respect for other people's symbols—their flags, their costumes, their objects of veneration—because in doing so we express regard for them. We expect the same in return. On that reciprocity is based the hope for peace.

On an island such as ours, the infrequent contact with people of vastly different traditions and values makes us susceptible to intolerance. We are not used to hearing languages other than Spanish and English; we are not familiar with non-Christian religions; we don't understand political institutions different from ours; and we laugh at the ways other nations dress, eat, or amuse themselves.

We have little patience with the past, too. As was stated in the introduction to the film *The Go-Between*, "The past is a foreign country: they do things differently there." And because the Puerto Rico of 60 or 100 years ago is so different from ours, we unconsciously tend to reject any of it that may have survived into our own days. This lack of tolerance for the symbols of previous generations has created havoc with our study of history. Records of municipal assemblies, like those of Morovis, hardly go beyond the present generation. Precious materials for social history, like the payrolls of *haciendas* or the correspondence between political figures, are burned every year by indifferent heirs. To this day we lack a good scholarly history of the period from 1898 to 1952; the work of stray American social and political scientists is often used to plug up the gap.

This indifference to our immediate past negates our own aspirations to establish our collective identity and sense of purpose. Sometimes we behave as if we were a bunch of families marooned by history on an island and we had nothing in common with each other but the discomforts of shipwreck. Only to the degree that we acquire a sense of perspective and see how we have become a people can we hope to develop tools to rescue ourselves from our mutual alienation. We won't recognize each other in the role of brothers until we develop consensus on the symbols of brotherhood. Otherwise we run the risk of tearing each other to pieces for the sake of a rose or an iota.

41. The Great Dominion of Canada
(February 14, 1974)

Amado Nervo wrote a great story about a girl who attempts to frighten her younger playmates with the warning that The Great Dominion of Canada is going to visit them that night. She dresses herself in increasingly more grotesque costumes. When the kids ask each terrible monster who he is, the monster answers that he is the third attendant or the second chamberlain of The Great Dominion of Canada. But in the end The Great Dominion doesn't show up; nothing could possibly match the expectations aroused.

I always think of The Great Dominion of Canada when I read the headlines in *Claridad* (the Socialist weekly). Crisis succeeds crisis; the denouement seems imminent; the situation can't possibly go beyond this week. But somehow total disaster eludes us, and professionals and retailers continue offering their services in *Claridad*'s ads with few apocalyptic forebodings evident.

But, of course, *Claridad* can muster its readers' attention each time because it has the knack of taking itself and nothing else seriously. In every issue it applauds a public figure and denounces a public villain, and it is the secret hope of every liberal in the land to be applauded once, just once, by *Claridad*. Then there is the centerfold, which, when Camero took pictures for it, was the best photographic display with social content in any paper on the island. In every issue it would take readers to a forgotten barrio or town, so that you could almost smell the open sewers and listen to fragile old ladies' stories about forgotten political promises. That centerfold alone was worth the ten cents. They still have it, but it has lost some of the punch. There are too many people in the photos and attention wanders. Then there are the columns. When Juan Mari Bras is on and has no particular ax to grind, he's worth your time. When he is off, he's no worse than some of our more revered public commentators.

But one can read *Claridad* every week and still think of Amado Nervo's Great Dominion of Canada. And perhaps one has to come to this mountaintop in Cayey and rid oneself of the inhibitions that hinder one from saying so. It is as if a certain glibness had overtaken *Claridad,* a certain privately shared comfort that its contributors belonged to an inner circle of the saved which the millennium would find unsullied by any bourgeois taint. One doesn't think so much of smugness as of that satisfied smile a third grader may have for being the only one in the class to have kept quiet while the teacher was out. It's the doctrinaire part of the self-assurance, the sort of presupposition that if one throws around enough orthodox Marxist-`
Leninist jargon and goes to the right picket line one has done one's bit. And for someone profane in such matters it's like being locked out—*omnes pagani exeant* (let all unbelievers depart). Have they then abandoned all hope?

If you compare the gist of *Claridad*'s biweekly message with that of the Governor's Message to the Legislature (and I can almost hear both sides vigorously disclaiming that there are any possible grounds for comparison), you may feel that both present a bleak prospect of our present situation, but both see some grounds of hope. They don't coincide on what is wrong and what is going to fix it, but there is some film of humanism in the concern of both: crypto-Christian in *Claridad*'s case and post-Utopian in the Governor's. And the humanistic concern of both has this in common, that it hasn't awakened the commensurate public response that the issues involved demand.

Somehow the system is not working, and while one team is trying to wreck it and the other is trying to fix it, the vast majority of us remain idle spectators, now passing off a rumor, now shrugging off a calamity. Maybe we should take stock of the situation, not because the Great Dominion may come but because we may spend the rest of our lives dreading it.

42. A Rage of Referenda
(September 23, 1974)

When the Popular Democratic Party regained the governorship in the elections of 1972, some party militants pushed to separate Río Piedras from San Juan, in order to weaken Carlos Romero Barceló, the New Progressive Party's mayor of San Juan. In 1974 this movement gained adherents from old loyalists from Río Piedras, who lamented that the municipality had been annexed to San Juan in 1951. Although no friend of the mayor, I thought the only way of resisting the dismemberment of the capital was by pushing local loyalties to the limits.

Then there came the time when Santurce became again an independent municipality. City Hall was by the church of San Mateo, and the municipal cemetery on the green spaces on Baldorioty de Castro Expressway. The city dump was under Martín Peña bridge. A brand new municipal sports center in Minillas featured a bowling alley, four tables for playing domino, and a volleyball net that could be stretched across De Diego Avenue between 2 and 4 in the morning.

Everybody thought that with the secession of Santurce from San Juan local pride had been satisfied. Unfortunately, at the inauguration of the mayor of Santurce the Miramar delegation received back row tickets, and soon afterwards the Miramar Liberation Movement demanded a referendum, for Miramarinos only, on the separate incorporation of their neighborhood. The MLM pointed out that Miramar contributed far more to Santurce than it received in services, and that the mayor seldom took the bus down Ponce de Leon avenue to see them.

It was thought that the independence of Miramar could be safely ignored, but a maverick city councilman from Villa Palmeras forged

113

a coalition with Parada 15 and Eduardo Conde political bosses and obtained simultaneous referenda for their localities. To everybody's surprise all separatist movements won at the polls. These victories forced Condado and Barrio Obrero to become municipalities too, since the Santurce sanitation trucks weren't allowed to go through other people's city limits.

Fernández Juncos then protested that Calle Loíza was getting the lion's share of municipal band concerts, but by that time Eduardo Conde had appropriated the city hall at San Mateo, thus forcing the birth of a municipality from San Jorge to Llorens Torres. The municipal band was split, Fernandez Juncos obtaining the oboe, the guacharo, and one clarinet, and Calle Loíza the flute and two drummers. The rest of the band went home to Aibonito, which was then reviving its claim to be the capital of Puerto Rico.

Santurce, being reduced to Parada 26 and Sagrado Corazon, by this time received the federal grant to build a monument to the American Revolution that it had solicited 18 months before. Since it was a sizable sum, the mayor went ahead with construction plans, and a huge statue of Patrick Henry asking for liberty or death was built on the only available site, the city's parking lot by Charneco. This move so aggravated city employees commuting from Las Madres that a fratricidal campaign developed to split the municipality.

Meanwhile Condado and Miramar were conducting naval warfare on the lagoon over dumping rights, and Playita was asking the United Nations to recognize its right of self-determination and independence from Villa Palmeras. The Pope complicated the situation by making Parada 15 a separate diocese, not realizing that Parada 19 had a prior claim based on cultic precedence. To top it all off, Fernandez Juncos obtained an atom bomb on loan from a Third World power, and things would have been grim indeed if the Eduardo Conde vice squad hadn't purloined it and dropped it on Ponce.

By this time a tourist slump had severely handicapped Calle Loíza's fiscal capacity. Its mayor, in a bright moment, negotiated commonwealth status with Culebra, by this time rich in the philatelic business on account of its LSD-gummed postage stamps. Calle

Loíza's move was ridiculed by its sister municipalities, and Eduardo Conde threatened invasion. Happily, the Culebra fleet appeared off Ocean Park and threatened to shell everything from Calle Calma to San Mateo. Thus peace was restored, and Calle Loíza people could celebrate without anxiety the feast of their patron saint, San Cocho.

43. A Letter to Javariz
(October 12, 1974)

Jorge Javariz was a columnist at the Spanish daily El Mundo, *and I had got into a controversy with him on account of the climate of intolerance that had prevailed in those years. Nowadays one tends to forget that these things happened.*

Don Jorge:

It is almost a year since you affirmed, in answer to one of my columns, that Puerto Rico is the most tolerant place on earth.

Since then:

1. Members of *Claridad's* staff were assaulted by nightriders who haven't been brought to trial.

2. "Controversial" artists found out that they were no longer welcome in the studios of WAPA TV.

3. The consulates of Argentina, Perú, and Venezuela have been bombed.

4. The chancellor of the University of Puerto Rico at Río Piedras was physically assaulted one morning while on his way to his office, and two centrist professors in the Social Sciences College have been harassed.

5. Several dozen professors at the University have been fired. Most of them are known to hold pro-independence views. Although budgetary reasons were adduced for the nonrenewal of contracts, in several instances replacements seem to have been found.

6. There was an attempt to bomb the Colegio de Abogados.

7. A study has revealed that some firms discriminate in their hiring practices against women and dark-skinned Puerto Ricans.

8. The offices of *Avance* magazine were destroyed by a bomb.

9. The house of vice-speaker Severo Colberg was pelted with stones.

10. Tenure was denied to a liberal philosophy professor at the Catholic University in Ponce "because he was a Cuban." Student leaders supporting him faced suspension.

11. Two more theaters have been knocked out by bombs.

12. Previous bombing incidents—the fourth floor of the Social Sciences graduate building at the UPR Río Piedras campus, the cars destroyed in the stadium parking lot during the game in which a visiting Cuban team participated, other attacks on *Claridad,* etc.—have remained unsolved.

I am sure that with weighty words and learned instances you can explain away all of these. You may dismiss some of the items because they have occurred only once, and the rest because they happen all the time and everywhere. Some you can attribute to extremists not representative of our society, and the rest to society's defense against the menaces of extremists.

Still I am not at peace. It may be that the very liberty I take in pointing out these instances of intolerance to you I may have to account for with my job or my life. One doesn't know these days.

But if nobody cries out that the emperor has no clothes on, we may continue playing out the farce that in this "most tolerant of countries" anyone can express an opinion or attend a meeting or activity without fear of violence. How can we say that we are free when we live in fear?

It doesn't matter if one's personal views are more in accordance with those usually expressed in your column than with those of most of the people who have been the victims of intolerance in recent months. To the extent that anybody in Puerto Rico is the victim of prejudice and intolerance, the liberty of each one of us is curtailed.

Part VI

Past Imperfect

44. San Guibin's Day

(November 28, 1974)

Art Buchwald used to publish every year a column explaining Thanks-giving to the French. I attempted to do the same thing with San Guibin, the Puerto Rican version of Thanksgiving, but someone wrote to the Editor saying that I, a Catholic, was being disrespectful to the tradition and the Pilgrim forbears who had escaped from England to New England. Fortunately, somebody else wrote to the Editor and pointed out that the Pilgrims were fleeing from Protestant King James I. But I was so discouraged that I quit writing San Guibin columns. This is my favorite.

Saint Guibin is busy. It is his day, which is only celebrated in Puerto Rico. He gets up early in the morning, has honey with his cereal, goes bicycling around heaven, and stops for lunch at Saint Peter's. There a brand new saint from the Third World, ignorant of such matters, raises the innocent question:

"Tell me, San Guibin, why do they celebrate your feast in Puerto Rico?"

Saint Peter groans because he has heard the answer hundreds of times, and he shuffles off on the excuse that there is a new batch of victims of the Brazilian police to attend to. But San Guibin loves to be asked the question. He refills his glass of ambrosia, settles back in his armchair, and begins:

"You know, of course, where Puerto Rico is. If not, I think you can get a good view from the kitchen window. Well, some 250 years ago, there was a terrible hurricane followed by famine and plague in Puerto Rico. A lot of people died. Of course, heaven wasn't prepared for such a massive influx of Puerto Ricans. You see, it was all right to have one or two in every now and then, but this was a sizeable crowd. So Saint Peter went to the door and interviewed the first batch:

'How many of you are baptized?'

"Everybody raised his or her hand. Saint Peter checked the next item on his tally sheet.

'Have you being going to church regularly?'

"There was a pause and then the Puerto Ricans in the group began to discuss among themselves. Finally an old *jibaro* with a hoe spoke up.

'With your honor's permission, we haven't gone to church too frequently.'

'Well,' said Saint Peter, 'I'm afraid we will not be able to put you up.'

"He was about to close the door, but the *jibaro* put his hoe in between. 'Your honor,' the old *jibaro* said, 'they took care of orphans. No one stopped by any of their houses who wasn't invited in for lunch. They stayed up with the sick, and that's why some of them caught the plague. They helped to hide runaway slaves.'

'That's all to the good,' said Saint Peter, 'but what about going to church?'

'Your honor must consider that we lived on the hills and there are not too many churches in Puerto Rico.'

'What!' said Saint Peter, 'I can at least see ten from where I am standing.'

'But it is a big island,' said the *jibaro*, and there are no roads.'

'Then you should have lived close to the churches, as the Laws of Indies say.'

'With your honor's pardon,' said the *jibaro*, 'most of the valley land is taken by the cattle people, and it's on the hills that you can get a *finquita* (little farm) and raise some chickens.'

'The Third Commandment, the Fourth Lateran Council, and the Council of Trent say,' began Saint Peter. But at this point Our Lady passed by, and an old woman waved to her: 'The Virgin! Hey! The Virgin!' Whereupon the whole group started shouting, clapping and whistling.

'Wait a minute,' said Saint Peter indignantly. 'You are still outside, and in any case that's no way to address such an important member of the celestial court.' But his words were lost because by now the group was paying no attention to him. Moreover the Lady was sending an angel to inquire about the commotion.

'Tell her it's a routine case of not going to church,' said Saint Peter, who didn't much like this meddling by a woman.

"The *jibaro*, however, tripped up the angel with his hoe, and while helping him to get up whispered: 'Tell her we are from Puerto Rico.'

"Well, the upshot of it was that the Virgin admitted the whole group, and by the front door, too. Saint Peter was on the verge of resigning his job, and it took a few fried fish dinners to put him back in humor. To attend to such cases in the future the *jibaro* with the hoe was deputized. And that's me," said San Guibin, "and that's why they celebrate my day in Puerto Rico."

45. Chronology of an *Asalto*
(December 26, 1974)

Asalto *is what a group of Christmas revelers used to perpetrate on sleeping friends and relatives during that long season stretching from Thanksgiving into deep January. In San Juan it was in its heyday in the 1970s. As you would move from one house to the next picking up people along the way, the owners of an "assaulted" home did not necessarily know many of the midnight carolers. In San Juan the custom has died down on account of the proliferation of gated subdivisions and the prevalence of security devices.*

At twenty to two the first car stopped in front of the target house, and Cuatro predicted that the other three cars had got lost. Trumpet suggested that they had been ticketed for speeding. Everybody got out to stretch, and someone sneezed.

"Keep quiet until they get here," said the First Driver.

"It's beginning to rain," grumbled Trumpet.

The dog came to the front garden and started barking. "He's going to jump the fence and bite us," whispered Trumpet. They all got back into the car.

Wife woke up Husband: "Someone's outside."

"Tomorrow I'll check it."

"I think I heard voices."

"The kids are watching the late show."

"They aren't. They are at a party."

"They'll get back all right, don't worry."

"That's not what I'm worrying about."

"Good," said Husband, and he fell asleep again.

At five after two the second car pulled up.

124

"Whatever happened?" asked the First Driver.

"Stopped at my cousin's along the way," said the Second Driver. "They are coming too. Anyone in there?"

"A dog."

The dog started barking again. The other cars arrived.

"Quiet everyone," stage-whispered the First Driver. "Let's gather in a bunch."

The dog jumped the wall and everybody scrambled for the cars.

"Does anyone know the dog?" asked the First Driver.

"It's all right," said Maracas, "I know all about dogs. He won't bite."

"Let's get the thing started," pleaded Trumpet.

"All right, O.K. Now let's get organized."

Wife woke up Husband again. "There are people outside."

"You are hearing things again."

At that moment the cacophony started: "*Saludos, saludos.*?

"It's an *asalto,*? said Wife.

"Next door."

"It can't be. They are at Rincón for the weekend."

"I told you we couldn't afford Rincón."

"I think it's here."

"No, the guys from the office came last week, and your brother's car is busted."

"Maybe friends of the kids."

"They were all at the same party. It's probably two houses down."

Outside they were singing "*De la montaña venimos.*?

"It's here all right," groaned Husband and got up.

"I don't have anything," panicked Wife.

All the neighborhood dogs were barking. "Maybe they are out," said Guicharo.

"The car is here," observed Palitos.

Cuatro started playing "*Abranme la puerta.*"

The door opened. "Come in, come in," said Wife.

They danced in. Husband said that he only had beer. The drivers asked for coffee. Wife suggested pancakes, and two or three people went into the kitchen with her. Cuatro, Guicharo, and Palitos began playing *plenas,* and soon they were shouting *bombas* in the living room. Husband came and danced with Wife in the kitchen. They had pancakes with sausages and hot chocolate with marshmallows. They formed a train and went choo-chooing around the backyard. It was a great party. Wife wanted to go with them to the next house, but she remembered that the kids were out, so they stayed.

The First Driver rounded up everybody. Trumpet had fallen asleep in front of the TV set and had to be roused. They left for Guicharo's brother's house.

"Well, your cousin certainly knows how to liven up a party," said Husband to Wife. "But he has aged."

"What cousin?" asked Wife.

"The one with the *cuatro*.?

"That wasn't my cousin. I thought he was the fellow who helps you coach the parish softball team."

"But that was the only person I thought I knew."

"Who were they, then?"

"Maybe the kids' teachers."

In one of the cars Palitos was saying, "You have nice in-laws."

"In-laws?" said Cuatro. "Never saw them before in my life. They must be relatives of the girl with glasses in the other car."

46. Bus Riding in Prose and Poetry
(June 20, 1975)

When I started going to the Archivo General three times a week by bus, to do my research on the history of Utuado, I found creative ways to spend the time during the ride. This was the fruit of one of those exercises.

This is how different authors would have expressed themselves on the subject of riding bus no. 2 at 5 p.m. on a rainy afternoon:

Thomas Wolfe: "What is it that we know so well and cannot speak? We do not know. All that we know is that we lack a tongue that could reveal, a language that could perfectly express the wild fury we know so well and cannot speak! All that we know is that the Stop 18 intersection is hopelessly clogged, and that there is still Stop 22 to pass, where some Volkswagened secretary will attempt to hold the traffic hordes with her puny vehicle. This is the way the world goes—with a blocked intersection, a dash, and another jam."

Henry James: "The very quality of the agglomeration around the middle of the bus, with those striving yet to acquire a sure holding finding themselves jolted by the sudden surge of concern for the lady with the suffocating child, diffused any attempt to discern in each individual passenger the motive for his or her being there at all."

William Shakespeare: "Fair cousin,
Cling to the rude ribs of this ancient carcass,
For sudden stops are all too probable;
Ere you know it your chin would sail past

That matron's ear and cleave her baby's lollipop,
Nor would it stop there, but seek a nest
In her crony's hair and thus embedded
Dislodge no little dandruff from her fallow locks."

G.K. Chesterton: "Brazen horns are blaring from some
    twenty blocks away;
All the Cadillacs have stopped, all the Chevvies are immobile;
Forty times the red has changed, forty times to no avail;
In the middle stands a truck, and across it a limousine;
But Bus No. 2 is Going to San Juan."

Flannery O'Connor: "'Don't!' the driver said, but she had started her sermon. "Listen Puerto Rico, listen Villa Palmeras, listen well Lloréns Torres and Calle Loíza! The world is going to disintegrate. Each wheel will go its separate way, one to the East and one to the West, and one to where the turtles swim in the open sea. We are like the wheels of this bus, yes sir, we are like those wheels. For when that day comes, some of us will go North and freeze, and some of us will go East and burn."

'Myself, I'm going to Eduardo Conde,'" a fellow shouted from the *cocina.*
'And so you will, *condenao,* so you will,' said the preacher."

47. Mrs. Ponce de León
(August 7, 1975)

My cousin Isabel Picó was a member of a team of scholars who reviewed the textbooks used in public schools and determined that they had to be overhauled on account of their gender bias. This column was a gentle spoof.

According to a recent article, history textbooks are being revised to erase the slightest sign of anti-female bias in them. As a contribution to the expurgation of any Puerto Rican history book that may suffer from male chauvinism, here is the lost and recently recovered record of a historical conversation. The place is Caparra, the time 1519.

Juan Ponce de León: "There is one more thing, dear. I think I'm going again to Florida this winter."

Mrs. Ponce: "Over my dead body you will."

Ponce: "But I'm getting on in years. And if I don't use my title of *Adelantado,* one of those Columbus fellows is going to get into my territory."

Mrs. Ponce: "No, sir. You are always running away from things, and you leave me with the mess you have made."

Ponce: "Now, come on, Leonor. Didn't I build you the stone house I promised you when you came over from Higuey? And isn't it the only stone house in town?"

Mrs. Ponce: "Sure it is. Next thing you know all the neighbors will be moving to that nice spot in the bay and we'll be left here all by ourselves."

Ponce: "Didn't you get your very own share of the gold mined?"

Mrs. Ponce: "Sure I did, and a lot of good it did to me. What can you buy in this place beside *yuca* (casave) from the Toa plantation?

No sir, if we are going any place, let's go to Spain. Or let's see Italy. I've never been there."

Ponce: "That's out of the question, Leonor. I must get back to Florida."

Mrs. Ponce: "I don't know what drags you there. You only found swamps the other time."

Ponce: "I *discovered* the Bahamas passage."

Mrs. Ponce: "Big deal. Meanwhile the Caribs were trying to burn this town. I had to take care of the children and the household while you were making yourself the biggest fool in Christendom looking for that fountain."

Ponce: "Now, let's not start up again about the Fountain."

Mrs. Ponce: "Other conquistadors look for sensible things. They bring back gold, slaves, birds, curiosities. I'm the only wife of a conquistador who gets nothing but stories."

Ponce: "Come on, honey, you are being mean. I did conquer this island, didn't I? I made you first lady here, didn't I?"

Mrs. Ponce: "And how long did that last? You let yourself be bounced out by Columbus's kid. Right now, we are nothing. I don't know how we are going to find husbands for María and Isabel."

Ponce: "I am the *Adelantado* of Florida and Bimini. All I need is a chance to get there again. I'll find the gold. We'll build a town. We'll be governors again. There'll be husbands for our daughters."

Mrs. Ponce: "Well, you go ahead, but I warn you, I'm through with moving. I don't want my furniture on a boat going to some mosquito-infested island."

Ponce: "You'll see how nice the climate is in Florida. And it's a big island; it may even be a continent, for all I know. How would you like to be the first lady on a continent? And then, there's always the Fountain."

Mrs. Ponce: "Juan, for once be quiet and let me sleep. I have to get up early to see that the new Indian hand milks the cows properly."

48. On Slaves as Lenders
(September 20, 1975)

For some students of the history of slavery in Puerto Rico, one of the puzzling aspects of the institution is how individual slaves won their freedom before slavery was abolished in 1873. As Consuelo Vázquez Arce has shown in a research paper on Naguabo published in *Anales de Investigación Histórica* and as other researchers are discovering about other areas of the island, a majority of emancipated slaves bought their freedom from their masters. The question is, then, how did they get the money to buy their freedom?

In his history of black slavery in Puerto Rico, Luis Díaz Soler sums up the statutes that prescribed that every slave owner should yield some land so that his slaves might work it in their spare time and save money for their redemption. But even in the most favorable of conditions, the cash yield of crops such as pumpkins, *yautías,* sweet potatoes and other roots, vegetables, and fruits would be too meager compared with the sum needed for buying their freedom. More profitable crops demanded either intensive care, which an non-free man toiling for his master's benefit six days a week from dawn to sunset could not provide, or prime cleared land, which his master was not likely to spare. Yet slaves did make money, as many individual emancipation acts show, and tips and *aguinaldos* (Christmastime gifts) cannot account for the three, four, or six hundred pesos needed, sums equivalent to the price for two or three hundred *cuerdas* of good uncleared land.

In 1973 in the course of a forum commemorating the centennial of emancipation, Benjamín Nistal cited evidence from Manatí which indicated that slaves there made money by raising a few heads of cattle, pigs, and poultry. He also referred to a lawsuit brought by a slave against a free person for the repayment of a loan. Nistal suggested that these two forms of economic activity—stock raising and money lending—may have helped slaves considerably on their way to freedom

Although my own research on the history of Utuado in the first half of the 19th century is still rudimentary, several documents concerning slaves there have called my attention to the role slaves may have played in Utuado's credit system. As several historians have underlined, 19th-century Puerto Rico had a severe monetary problem. Coinage tended to leave the island. Most affected were inland towns like Utuado, where in the 1820's the municipal government unsuccessfully petitioned the *Intendencia* (Treasury) for permission to pay taxes in kind, because there was not enough money circulating locally. From the 1830's to the 1860's in many Utuado notarial acts it is stated that the price of land bought is paid for in cattle or quantities of coffee or rice. In notarial acts surviving from some years during this period I have found acknowledgment of debts to seven slaves.

In one of the acts, the dying slaveowner states in his last will that he owes twenty-four pesos to one of his slaves for two *fanegas* of coffee. But what seems interesting is that six other slaves are creditors not of their masters but of some other free person. Antonio Agustín has loaned to the local brickmaker a sum which over the years has generated interest, and the total owed has amounted to 144 pesos and 7 *maravedises*. Juan José has deposited 50 pesos with one of the wealthiest Utuado merchants, and interest has accumulated "at the usual rate." Carmen has raised cattle in partnership with Salvador Muñiz; she has sold her share of the herd to a landowner, who has held up payment. Interest has accumulated on the debt, and she is owed 332 pesos with 51 cents. Debts to two other slaves are acknowledged in two other retailers' wills, and the sixth slave, Felix, is owed 125 pesos by a resident of Arecibo.

These few cases suggest that in a society chronically short of money, such as Utuado, a segment of the population intent on saving provided merchants and artisans with some funds to finance business activities. One may surmise that slaves' capacity to generate savings and make these savings accessible for investment was one of their contributions to the development of Puerto Rico.

49. Six Thousand Utuadeños
(December 15, 1975)

This column tells the story of how I became interested in Utuado's history. I wound up writing five books on Utuado: Libertad y Servidumbre; Amargo Café; Los Gallos Peleados; 1898: La Guerra Después de la Guerra *(translated into English as* Puerto Rico 1898); *and* Los irrespetuosos.

My grandmother, Alvilda Sureda, was born in Utuado in 1887. During the last year of her life I spent every weekend I could at her house in Cayey. We talked of many things, and especially about old times. She was a great storyteller and had a magnificent sense of humor. If I had had any sense I would have taped her stories, or at least noted them down, but, of course, I thought we still had years of weeding and planting to do together, and in any case, she would have scoffed at the idea of my writing down what she said.

Although beset by all the ills of her great age, she retained her flair for planning. "Wait until I feel better and we'll ask your uncle to take us to Utuado. I would like you to see it. You know, once in Germany I told people it was the most beautiful place in the world. Afterwards your grandfather laughed at me, saying that I boasted of Utuado as if I didn't know it was the place where the devil got off when he visited Puerto Rico. Buy you'll see."

Well, we never got to Utuado, and it was probably a good thing, because the town has changed. But after her death I wondered what kind of memorial I should create to her. It occurred to me that since history is my craft maybe I should try writing a history of Utuado. True, there are already several good works on Utuado's history by Francisco Ramos, Pedro Hernández Paralitici, Carlos Seijo, and Julio

Martínez Mirabal, and there is an interesting 19th-century book, *El Porvenir de Utuado*, by Ramón Morel Campos, as well as Esperanza Mayol's splendid recent autobiography. But these writers didn't have access to the materials that the Archivo General de Puerto Rico has now assembled, and they scarcely touched on the first century of the town's existence.

"Of the history of Utuado before 1855," one of its chroniclers wrote, "little is known." But fragmentary information gathered so far on 6,000 Utuadeños has thrown a fair amount of light on that early period. One can follow families whose first representatives moved inland from Arecivo, Ponce, San Germán, and Aguada and clustered around the town site and Arenas and along the two broad rivers, Viví and Grande. They had floods then, too, and epidemics followed. In the course of a decade families lost six or seven children, so that only one or two would live to carry on the surname. The settlers struggled against the mountains, which barred the way to the port; against the lush vegetation, which crept upon the planted areas and isolated each family from its neighbors; against the hurricanes, which in a few hours destroyed a decade's efforts to build up a herd or a coffee plantation. Then a smug outsider, like Iñigo Abad or Miyares, would come and sum up the harsh realities in a couple of patronizing sentences and move on, not understanding how much the little progress achieved had cost.

Thus, in that first century, those 6,000 Utuadeños lived and died, leaving the usual ink stains on official records, how much they paid or still owed in taxes. One can pounce upon traces of their quarrels and aspirations, or stagger under the heavy verbiage of their public officials. One hears of the pig that ate a neighbor's yams and caused a jurisdictional dispute with Arecibo, of the day the town was saved from burning down, or of Lares' nefarious plot to annex Barrio Angeles. And all these things, the weighty and the ludicrous, form part of the process by which that small, vulnerable community cleared the land, built roads, developed credit and markets, and established churches, schools, courts, and hospitals. Utuado became a city (its official designation since 1894), and its coffee crop was one of the island's most valuable assets. But that part of the story belongs to Utuado's chronicled period of elegance, when it had two newspapers, a theater, the island's second electrical plant, and a host of poets. That ephemeral heyday some, but very few, of the early 19th-century Utuadeños lived to see.

The history of Utuado has no cannons in it, no kings, few governors. But to study how Utuado was formed out of the prolonged dreams, toils, and heartbreaks of several thousand men and women is to understand, in an instant, that we are a people forged by history, not transients between New York-bound planes, caught on this island by the throw of dead diplomats' dice.

50. Voters of 1871
(February 9, 1976)

Historians often have trouble uncovering the opinions and attitudes of the average citizen of the past. In researching municipal history it is easier to run across minutes of speeches made by mayors and councilmen than to find records of what farmers, shoemakers, teachers, or government employees were thinking. It was therefore something of a surprise to read an 1870-71 Utuado electoral register that brims over with instances of the aphorisms and judgments of several hundred 19th-century Utuadeños.

The register was formed to enable residents of the municipality to prove that they could write and thus qualify as voters in the upcoming elections for the local *Diputación Provincial* (Provincial Assembly) and the island's deputies to the Spanish *Cortes* (Parliament). Since men who paid eight pesos or more in taxes automatically qualified, the register was intended only for those whose right to vote was based solely on their literacy. These voters were called *capacidades,* and although many of them were adult sons of the rich, most were presumed to come from the ranks of artisans and small proprietors. Thus Lidio Cruz Monclova, in his history of the period, cites the words of a Mayaguez conservative deploring the fact that the *capacidades*, by going to vote, had profaned the chairs of city hall, while the *Boletín Mercantil* expressed outrage that unworthy people were discussing reforms and public liberties.

In the 50-odd pages of the Utuado register some of these *capacidades'* opinions on current affairs are recorded. Each had to write a sentence and sign, and many used the occasion to protest about the state of the roads leading to their respective barrios. A thoughtful resident of Angeles even noted that if the river flooded over, he wouldn't be able to get home. There were also those who revealed considerable pride in their barrios. Agustín Martínez said that Angeles produced much coffee. Jerónimo Vázquez found Arenas beautiful. Benito Chevere said Tetuán was a *platanero,* a plantain producer. Manuel Cardona boasted of the uprightness of Caguana's people, but Isidoro Pérez complained that Bibí Arriba was the place where people did the least work. Immediately below, however, Dámaso Vélez replied that neither laziness nor forbidden games were tolerated there.

"I am a *jibaro,*" wrote Baldomero Martínez. "I am proud of it, and I am also a liberal." Others preferred to declare their moral convictions: "God rewards the just"; "Just as virtue is rewarded, the criminal is punished"; "Children are a piece of one's heart." Simeón Marín said that "true happiness consists in wishing to be what one is."

Although residents of the more distant barrios tended to write simple declarative sentences, some of those in or near towns took pleasure in showing off their skills with more complicated sentences. A resident of Bibí Abajo wrote: "In spite of the fact that this municipality has twenty thousand souls, it is quite possible that the number of those who can read and write won't reach five hundred." The son of the notary commented on how the foresight of governors contributed to the people's happiness, while a Spaniard declared: "France is going towards ruin on account of the internal conflicts that destroy its forces." Others made reference to the recently installed telegraph, to expected political reforms, to a smallpox epidemic, and to particularly heavy rains, while the son of one of the biggest landowners observed that "the police rules in force are, for the most part, inapplicable to the new needs which from day to day are arising in towns."

In many cases the orthography was poor, even poorer than that of students today. The calligraphy was hardly better. Some signatures curved upwards while others consisted of large block letters. One can easily imagine a prospective elector grasping a pen with calloused hands while trying to remember how once, long ago, he learned to make *z*'s or *j*'s.

51. Don Samuel Quiñones
(April 1, 1976)

My generation grew up knowing no other Senate president than the recently deceased Samuel Quiñones. Too young to remember Luis Muñoz Marín's fiery days in the Senate chamber, we went through grade school, high school, college, and even professional training with no other image of the Puerto Rican Senate presidency than that of the learned and talkative short man with a moustache. It was something of a start to return to Puerto Rico after years abroad and find in the post a man who was young enough to be his son.

Those of us who were students at San Ignacio around the same time as his oldest son and namesake remember don Samuel in a more familiar role. When we phoned his son, don Samuel was as likely as not to answer the phone himself. When we visited—and it was always open house at the Quiñones' home at Punta Las Marías—he might be there to open the door and bid us welcome. Many a ride we got on car No. 2.

We all knew don Samuel's interest in the preservation of the correct usage of Spanish in Puerto Rico, a subject on which we endlessly teased his son. But his intellectual interests were vast. On telling him after graduating from high school that I intended to major in history, he asked me whether I had read Toynbee's *Study of History.* I had never heard of Toynbee, so he warmly recommended his works to me. I still remember working up the courage in my first week of freshman year to ask someone on the library staff of Spring Hill College whether they had this book by Toynbee. "Which volume?" I was asked. Nonchalantly I answered, "The first." I had no idea the work could be so long. It was the first book I took out in college. I was certain that if he got the chance don Samuel would quiz me on it at Christmastime.

Don Samuel and his sensitive and gifted wife doña Clara Vizcarrondo had an unaffected but intense love for Puerto Rican history and culture. This happened in the Puerto Rico of the 1950's, when such things still evoked the suspicion of *independentismo*. For them there was no break between 19th- and turn-of-the-century writers and the contemporary scene, a link that current technocrats often miss. One can easily imagine that if don Samuel hadn't entered politics he would have still made a name for himself as a writer. Of his generation of *Populares* he was probably the purest intellectual, which may have removed him from the masses but certainly assured him the respect of his peers.

It was a loss that he didn't publish a volume of memories, a genre still badly underrepresented in Puerto Rican letters. The men of 1940, it is sad to see, are dying out, and in spite of all the printed speeches and political treatises that they leave behind, nothing could so thoroughly encapsulate their experiences for their juniors than their own written testimony.

It is said that we have an oral rather than a written culture; that in Puerto Rico it is more important to express oneself well than to write. Perhaps, then, an oral history project, well conceived and executed, might make more understandable for us the choices and priorities of that crucial generation.

52. Don Coco
(July 24, 1976)

My uncle Jorge Bauermeister, who teaches agricultural skills at Guavate penal camp, got permission to have me interview don Coco, Fernando Lucret Galarza, the composer of *plenas* and *trabalenguas* (tongue-twisters), who was turning 60 years old. Don Coco is a tall, strong, black man with lively eyes and a ready tongue. He is under a heavy prison sentence for homicide, and in recent years he has been serving it at the Guavate camp in Cayey.

"Do you know about the four winds in a *plena*?" he asked me, taking charge of the conversation.

I confessed that all I knew about *plenas* was what I had heard on the WIPR's Saturday evening program featuring José Luis Torregrosa and Paquito López Cruz.

"Well," he said, "few people nowadays know about the authentic *plena*. But ever since I was 13 I have been composing *plenas*. Of course, you don't compose one by sitting down and writing it out. It comes to you while the drums are throbbing and you are on the spot trying to work out a piece of news. The *plena* is above all a commentary on something that has happened, like the one I did about the dynamo wires between Ponce and San Juan. Many times the *plenero* forgets what he has composed the night before. But I remember and I have hundreds of *plenas* written out, many of them that no one has heard. Like this one about Ruth Fernández."

He sang it out. It had many verses about Ruth Fernández's singing in different places and being acclaimed.

"That's good," I said, "really good."

"It's one of many." And for the next hour don Coco sang snatches of his *plenas* and told about the circumstances of their composition.

"Have you heard the one, 'Donde estará la tumba de mi santa madre?' [Where would my sainted mother's tomb be?]? It is mine; I made it for a Mother's Day when López Victoria wanted something new. And do you know the one, 'Cuando las mujeres quieren a los hombres' [When women are in love with men]? I composed it. But it's not like the one they sing on the radio nowadays. It's long, it goes on and on." He sang some four or five verses of it, with mentions of wizards, cemeteries, and love potions. By now I was absorbed.

"He also wrote the one about Juana Morales," said my uncle.

"Was there a real Juana Morales?" I asked.

"Sure there was, just like there was a real Elena, who as a matter of fact was a *plenera.* But Juana Morales was a woman with a very quick temper. They don't sing it as I first sung it. You see, Juana Morales was a woman in Mayaguez who had a plot of land with several breadfruit trees. Youngsters would try to steal the breadfruits, so Juana would come and curse them out. She had a wicked tongue. So one time I was at a neighbor's place and someone was banging the drums and I was looking at Juana's place and it all came to me:

> *Bajo un palo de pana*
> *Vive Juana Morales*
> *Que es la única mujer*
> *Que me ha mentao la madre.*

> [Under a breadfruit tree
> Lives Juana Morales
> Who is the only woman
> who has slurred my mother's name.]

"They don't sing it that way now, of course, they changed the last verse to add the bit about eating *panas con aguacate* [breadfruit with avocado]."

"Do you still compose?"

"Sure I do. If I ever get out I would go and see some of my old friends to publish some of my *plenas.* I have one about someone standing in a prison courtyard and asking the leaves of a mango tree why he has ended up there. And one about fishermen, and another one about a baseball team we once had in my town, 'De Mayaguez las mesas,' and one about myself when I was at the Marina in San Juan. I have tongue-twisters too, like the one about 'El castillo de Cucurumbe.?? He proceeded to recite a part of this piece, which seemed challenging enough.

I didn't ask don Coco about how he had come to be serving such a long sentence, but it seemed a pity that someone so obviously talented should spend his old age at a penal camp without a chance to contribute his art to society.

Part VII

In the Time
of the Prodigals

53. The Prodigals
(August 14, 1976)

For years I resisted getting a driver's licence, so when I started going to the mountain town of Utuado to do historical research, I usually took a publico, *that is, a car that picks up and leaves passengers along an appointed route. I wish I had written down all the stories I heard on those rides, but this one day I had to share my ride with my readers.*

There's nothing like traveling by *publico* and bus around the island to learn what's going on. On August 4, on a trip to and from Utuado, I listened to the following conversations:

(a) Between Bayamón and Manatí, a runaway teenager explained to a university student why he had denounced his stepfather to the police, why he himself got into fights so often at school, and what he planned to do now that he was on his own.

(b) Between Arecibo and Utuado, the subject was births. A *jíbaro* father of fifteen said all of his children gave no trouble at birth, except the one who was born by caesarean.

"He has become a *bandolero.* Booze and fights."

"It must have been the anesthesia," said a sympathetic lady.

"When he is not drinking he's all sweetness. But once he starts, he smashes everything in sight. You have to get eight or ten people together and tie him. The other day he broke all the windows of his younger brother's car and slashed the four tires. But the Good Lord took care of it, for the following day arrived this ticket from the farmer for whom we have worked in New York. So he left, and the bandit, it's six weeks ago and he hasn't written a word."

"It must have been the anesthesia," said the woman with deepened conviction.

"We old people don't want our children to send us money. We only want to know how they are, if they need anything."

"The anesthesia," the woman said, "must have got to his nerves."

(c) Between Utuado and Arecibo, Ismael, the bus driver, explained his running feud with an old man.

"Twenty minutes before the bus is due to leave he gets on with two pigs. I tell him he can't bring them on. 'I'll give you four dollars,' he says. 'Not for 25,' I tell him. 'I'll put them in a sack,' he says. 'They would still stink up the bus,' I tell him. 'Then I won't take the bus ever again,' he says. But can you imagine—suppose some guy from the Public Service Commission caught me carrying pigs on this bus. What would happen then? *No se puede enborujar lechones con gente* (You can't mix pigs with people)."

He looks around for approval. "Now, if it had been hens, that's another story."

(d) Between Arecibo and Manatí, a recent arrival from New York City told of his search for his 17-year-old brother who had slipped away from their stepmother's house four days ago.

"I went to the Cantera of Ponce. Yesterday afternoon I went to Adjuntas; they had seen him the day before. I didn't sleep last night, spent it talking and drinking beer. My cousin in Manatí phoned his girlfriend's family in Caguas, but they hadn't seen him. Now, why would he do something like that? In New York he was very religious. I was too, you know. For three years. I belonged to this Pentecostal Church of the Good Samaritan. Those were the best years of my life. When you are into this Christian thing you feel all right inside."

(e) Between Vega Baja and Vega Alta, three other recent arrivals compared life in New York and here.

"Hair stylists here don't do things the way you tell them. Like in New York City, man, *tu ibas a un hairstylist y por 16 pesos te hacía blond* (you went to a hair stylist and for $16 he made a blond of you)."

54. Let's Not Confuse Training, Education
(January 18, 1977)

This is an issue that keeps coming back in educational debates in Puerto Rico.

Just as folklore and culture are not synonymous, neither are training and education identical. In Puerto Rico, however, these terms tend to be confused. Whenever the current needs of the job market are underlined, somebody always points out that the educational system is not providing for those needs. If the critic is iconoclastic he will say that what is needed are fewer readers of Plato and more welders or computer programmers. If he is trying to reflect practicality he will only say that admission to the university system is wasted on thousands of applicants who will never derive material profit from their higher education.

The implication, in either case, seems to be that a university education is a means to acquire credentials for a professional job. Wherever that technocratic presupposition has appeared, from the Soviet Union to Africa, it has distorted the debate on university curricula. Obviously, you don't need Plato to program a computer—but only those with a philosophical background will understand why none but a civilization that had been nurtured by Plato could devise Fortran. A society whose life is organized by computers can be run by technicians who have read Plato in anthologies, or not at all. But without great numbers of persons who have been trained to think about the larger questions, the computerized society will degenerate into a sybaritic technocracy, where any means can be justifiably programmed to achieve broadly accepted ends.

The technocrat, of course, will point out that his priorities in high-

147

er education don't exclude traditional university subjects, but would only limit them to those whose vocational aptitudes destine them to perpetuate the species of social science and humanities professors. He may even point out that in previous centuries only a miniscule portion of Western Europeans enjoyed the privilege of studying those classics which educators today would discuss with all comers.

But what may have happened in the select universities of baroque Europe at one time reflected the social and political systems then predominant. Societies run on the basis of privilege, like 18th-century Venice or Georgian England, need only several hundred educated persons to manage their affairs. True democracies, however, can only be preserved where the public is moved by something other than slogans and jingles—in other words, where citizens have been educated to think for themselves.

When people can't distinguish between what is right and wrong, what is beautiful or ugly, what is true or false, but propaganda and fashion dictate every turn, then votes can be bought or sold, and long-range changes may be brought about by slick publicity stunts.

To tell people that learning to weld constitutes an education is but the first step toward convincing them that having a job is more important than knowing their rights, or in the notorious words of the 1930's, that *Arbeit Macht Frei*, work makes one free. I, for one, prefer John 8:32, *The truth shall make you free.*

55. Letter from Port-au-Prince
(June 18, 1977)

To celebrate my cousin Francisco's college graduation, we went for a
week to Haiti. We leased a Volky and drove all over Haiti, gathering
marvelous memories. On our return I wrote the following.

One could say that Haiti is an enormous workshop supported by
the churches and international aid agencies for the benefit of half a
dozen concerns, the most visible of which is the presidential family,
but like every other exaggeration it risks overstating the core issue and
mangling the tenuous links with sanity which significant exceptions
provide. Here it becomes exasperating to observe the contradiction
between the vast amounts of energy spent daily by five million people constantly on the move and the meager yield of such efforts in
terms of human living standards. But rather than moralize on the
obvious scandal of having so many hungry people one hour away
from the wasteful kitchens of San Juan, one should rather attempt to
draw the potential lesson in the contrast between Haiti and Puerto
Rico.

In a way Haiti is a picture of what Puerto Rico could have been if
18th-century Spain had sponsored the intensive exploitation of the
land that France attempted here. Puerto Rico is lucky to have been
then a backwater of history. To clear the vast tropical forests of western Hispaniola, the French plucked half a million slaves out of Africa
and, at an immense cost in human suffering, by 1788 they were
exporting, according to Charles Frostin, 35 thousand tons of white
and 46 thousand tons of brown sugar and some 77 million pounds of
coffee. This was then the most prosperous colony in the world.

The slave revolution that destroyed this profitable exploitation was the last in a chain of movements of resistance by different segments of the local free population against the metropolitan government. The collapse of the slave plantations, however, accelerated rather than mitigated the intensive abuse of the land which the French had inaugurated. Strip farming, goat grazing, and woodcutting for timber and charcoal peeled the greenness of the hills; erosion did the rest. You can travel today from Cap Haitien to Jacmel on fairly good roads, but you'll clamber everywhere over the tattering skulls of dead mountains. If Haiti is poor today it is because the land was sacked to fulfill short-term needs; they are living here in the 21st century, with all the doomsday predictions of ecologists come true.

Haitians probably work harder than Puerto Ricans, but their efforts yield less. Although their population density is not as heavy as ours, the country is more obviously over-populated in terms of the available resources. There is enough mission-sponsored medicine to keep millions walking the incredible distances that twice a week must be covered to take a couple of freshly woven baskets and the extra hen to market, but there is just not enough meat, milk, and eggs. The frequently observed redhaired children don't have Viking ancestors; they suffer from malnutrition.

We Puerto Ricans, however, should visit Haiti more often, not just to gape at the erosion (which in our own Jayuya already is making an impressive debut), but to learn from a hardworking people that material comfort is not the end-all of existence. For when everything is said and done, there is more beauty and serenity, more creativity and spontaneous laughter here than in the six cities that clutter the environs of the bay of San Juan.

56. The Coquification of Culture
(July 6, 1978)

Talk about an essay that pleased no one. On the left, some people told me I was being too soft on the statehooders. On the right, not too many weeks had passed after the publication of this column when a militant statehooder was named Executive Secretary of the Institute of Puerto Rican Culture. Culture wars ensued, but fortunately I was going to spend a year abroad, in Mexico.

A generation ago, statehooders were often suspected and by their own words often convicted of belittling Puerto Rican culture. An anthology could be compiled of statements of dubious taste in which one or other pro-statehood journalist, intellectual, or professional asked where the Puerto Rican Mozarts and Shakespeares were. The present governor himself (Carlos Romero Barceló), in a quotation which every now and then is taken out of context to harass him, is supposed to have stated some fifteen years ago that there was no such thing as Puerto Rican culture.

Things have indeed changed, but supporters of commonwealth and independence have seen fit to keep alive the image of the typical statehooder as someone uncritically Americanized and Americanizing who would gladly bulldoze half of Ponce to keep the other half commercially viable. They tend to forget how Romero, when he was mayor of San Juan, resisted pressures to wreck the Plaza de Armas, or how governor Ferré retained Ricardo Alegría as Executive Director of the Institute of Puerto Rican Culture when it would have been relatively easy to have had his head on a platter. In fact, it is one of the encouraging signs on the all too bleak Puerto Rican scene that one of the most politically sensitive areas, that of culture, has for so

151

long remained out of reach of partisan politics.

While the government has wisely refused to make a battleground of our cultural patrimony, others have moved in and taken up long neglected strands of our heritage. Advertising agencies, discarding the absurd Nordic motifs that constituted so much of their standard fare, and probably encouraged by the initial achievements of Young and Rubicam, have put to work a number of Puerto Rican themes on behalf of their clients. International civic groups, which not too long ago were perceived as instruments of cultural assimilation, have become the patrons of artisans, authors, and artists. Some banks have sponsored literary contests and painters'exhibitions. Churches and private schools have held festivals in which Puerto Rican culture is highlighted; younger professionals decorate their offices with the works of contemporary artists, and even department stores whose indifference to Puerto Rican arts and crafts was a byword have regularly scheduled Puerto Rican fortnights.

All this interest and patronage has naturally made a difference in the lives of some painters, woodcarvers, composers, writers, musicians, lithographers, and other artists. To have a retrospective show of Lorenzo Homar's work in the Museo de Ponce or to establish a yearly prize for the best doctoral dissertation in the UPR's Hispanic Studies department is indeed progress. The question is whether enough has been done and whether much of what is being done tends to slant patronage towards standardized folklore and away from the new creative art and literary forms.

It is absurd, naturally, to put in the same bag the simpering *coquis* in television ads and the efforts to revive our *Taíno* heritage through festivals, but there is a common line that runs through many of these manifestations of *criollismo,* and it makes one wonder. It is the deliberate partiality of the effort, the unuttered statement that only what is picturesque or certifiably dead needs to be pointed out. For every dubious account of *Taíno* bravery there are 30 documented instances of black defiance and courage, for every dead poet there are 50 loud and lunging ones struggling to be heard, for every curious and brittle piece of *jíbaro* craftmanship there are a hundred idle hands of art students waiting for the chance to fashion clay, metal, or wood in school where there are no art workshops. It is only the folklore tip of the culture iceberg that people seem to notice.

One wonders whether in the end the confusion will persist between folklore and culture. Like any other living group, from ancient sailors to stone age cave dwellers, we have a folklore, but that is not the sum total of our creative capacities. Puerto Rican culture is not *coquís* or *bacalaitos fritos* (codfish fritters), as some ingenuous mainlanders who want to prove that they belong here often presuppose, but rather it is what we continually think, write, sing, and in any way create and profoundly express about our changing situation as a people. It is not something one preserves, like an old flower pressed inside a book, or even fosters, like an exotic plant, but a force that will remain kaleidoscopically alive so long as we keep identifying ourselves as a people and not as a subspecies of some transoceanic genus. But if we confuse culture with folklore, if we *coquify* it, we run the risk of forgetting who we are and end up by dressing up for tourists who want a bit of local color.

57. Titina and the 50's
(January 27, 1979)

My uncle Jorge Bauermeister, one of the last few farmers remaining in Cayey, once wanted me to write a column on the mule Titina, which was then more than 30 years old and still as stubborn as the day he bought her. Although admitting that there might be a story in it, I never got around to writing it, perhaps suspecting that the last thing a harried Sanjuanero would want to read before hopping in his car and getting into the morning rush hour was a story of a mule that would let itself be roped in fewer than five minutes only on Sundays.

The mule has since died, and let it be said in favor of her reputation that when she put a day's work in, she fully justified the couple of hours spent in chasing her through brambles and *guayabales*. She was strong, sure-footed and remarkably good-tempered for one so addicted to roaming free. She wasn't one for dropping her load of bananas while crossing a stream or kicking you when she got the chance. All in all she belonged to that fabulous golden age which nowadays everyone evokes so freely, when Muñoz Marín was governor and you could buy a *piragua* for five cents.

It is a curious thing that the frontier of nostalgia in Puerto Rico has moved up relatively so close in time. When I was a kid, old people still talked about Spanish times, and middle-aged people about the 1920's and 30's, but in neither case was there much desire to revert back to those bygone days. One of my grandmother's most vivid childhood memories was the lack of bread in coffee-rich Utuado during the American blockade of 1898. As for the years between the San Felipe Hurricane and World War II, although everyone concerned might like his or her youth back, no one seemed to want to relive those difficult days. The good old days seemed to have been rather short, perhaps between 1910 and 1914, when coffee prices had some-what recovered from the plunge after 1900 and Europe hadn't been detected as unsafe for democracy. To a kid, that period seemed unrea-sonably remote; the age of Muñoz Rivera, De Diego, and Barbosa was already written about in books and there were statues of them in parks.

In any case we were being constantly told that good days were coming. You couldn't go to a movie without seeing a newsreel about a new factory being opened. The Caribe Hilton was supposed to be the eighth marvel of the world. The new road to Caguas was being built and that would put Cayey within a two-hour reach of Santurce. There were all kinds of blueprints in the air: the Isla Verde Interna-tional Airport, the 11-story high Professional Building, perhaps even a new baseball stadium.

All these projects may seem small change today, but at that time they were visible instances of how things were turning around for the better. Puerto Ricans had a lot of confidence in themselves then; we may have even proved to be a little tiresome to foreigners with our self-assurance and our peculiar brand of manifest destiny. We didn't have many Olympic medals to brag about, no beauty queen titles, no impressive per capita income, no air-conditioned shopping centers or expressways, no cardinal's hat, and no Condado tourist complex, and yet we walked around with more pride in ourselves than we do today.

More important, when it rained you took shelter on other people's porches, without provoking fear or resentment. Drugs were medica-tions they gave to wounded soldiers in movies; grills were artistic devices to allow young couples in Spain to pass carnations to and fro; and a professional career was something you undertook to be of ser-vice to your countrymen. We were awfully naive to have believed all these things, and to have underestimated the power of greed, frustra-tion, and selfishness.

We thought the good times required less hard work to preserve them. We settled for giving only half of our society a better life, pre-supposing that like an ink blot the good things would reach all in due time. The raised expectations weakened our moral commitments and made the fortunes of a few at the expense of the aspirations of the many. If we miss the 1950's, which weren't all that placid, it's because we have failed to raise our hopes for the 1980's.

58. A Visit to the Lord of Chalma
(July 18, 1979)

It was my last Sunday in Mexico, and I was groaning at how fast time had gone. I hadn't gone to Oaxaca, as I had once wished, or to the pyramids in Yucatan or the Campeche ruins. The history research project had nibbled away all my time there. I hadn't lived up to my visa status as a tourist. "This is awful," I told myself; "next *alborada* mass Raquel Helfeld is going to take me to task for having spent a whole school year in Mexico and seen so little."

Well, I had a whole Sunday with which to patch up my reputation as a traveler. I couldn't go far, so I decided to go to Chalma. "If you want to observe popular religiosity at close hand," a fellow Jesuit had told me, "you must go to Chalma."

"Is it more intense then than the Villa of Guadalupe?"

"Ever since they built the new basilica, the Villa hasn't been the same. The basilica is too modern, too functional. It serves to keep the sweating Indians from rubbing shoulders with the "proper" people, but it isn't a popular shrine in the same sense the old basilica was. Now Chalma is the real thing."

When I told someone at the house I was going to spend the Sunday in Chalma, he asked me, "Are you going to dance?"

"Dance?"

"One goes to Chalma to dance before the Lord. You get off before you reach the town, bathe yourself in a stream, put on a garland of flowers on your head, walk the last two miles to the shrine, and dance before the Lord of Chalma."

Well, I felt that to fulfill all these particulars might be a bit awkward, but I bought the bus ticket anyhow.

Chalma was not quite that simple. It rather reminded me sharply

157

that we priests know about popular religiosity what my esteemed colleagues in political science at the University of Puerto Rico know about party politics in Orocovis. It is true that many people walk the last couple of miles down to the shrine, but no one had told me about the bicycles. It is a sight to watch from the bus window one beribboned cyclist after the other riding the rather steep slope down towards Chalma. It brought to mind Quique Bird's story about how the Jesuit is prepared beforehand for the anticipated penance of doing several laps around heaven.

And yet at Chalma itself the atmosphere was one of reverent familiarity. Not having brought a garland of flowers, I felt the way I did the time I went to my first history graduate school meeting in Río Piedras without putting on a tie. There was something moving about seeing streams of men, women, and children, crowned with red, yellow, and white flowers, advancing through the marketplace towards the church. So the Aztecs, the chroniclers wrote, used to flock to their pyramids on solemn days.

At the church door the pilgrims surrendered their garlands. They are not allowed to approach the altar on their knees, though some do it. The Lord of Chalma is high on the main altar behind a panel of glass, a carved crucified Christ looking deader than in Velazquez' somber picture. The hopelessness of the corpse on the cross is a stark contrast to the hope in the eyes of the faithful who come to ask him for cures.

It was then that I realized that as a sightseer I was shamefully out of place before the Lord of Chalma. I had got too used to seeing Gothic cathedrals with the eyes of a historian. But my fellow pilgrims had much more serious concerns than discerning schools of art. The Lord of Chalma is reputed to be miraculous, and I felt like an outsider, someone who has come to court without a suit to press.

I supposed you had to be poor, devoid of any know-how except the one that is supposed to count here, so that you could talk to the Lord of Chalma, and, what is more important, feel that he had heard you out. I looked around—most of the pilgrims were young, eager Indians, poorly dressed. I was taller, heavier, paler than most of the people who knelt beside me. It is a strange sensation to be a witness to something authentic, rich, spontaneous, and feel that you are not a part of it.

At a side chapel a young priest was sprinkling the ever-pressing throng with holy water. I could never see myself, after so many years of study, doing something like that in a manner so patently and mechanically magical. Nearby, coins tinkled, and there was a brisk over-the-counter trade in pictures of the Lord of Chalma. One feared that at any minute John Calvin was going to storm in and start overturning things. But I wasn't shocked. Everything was as natural as buying peace dove buttons at last decade's anti-war rallies.

It seems that nowadays no one is allowed to dance before the Lord of Chalma, or perhaps the prohibition is enforced just on Sundays. But the ritual bath takes place in the stream that runs beside the church. It is a joyous, splashy affair, more reminiscent of *Godspell* than of the Jordan baptisms in the usual Holy Week movies. And perhaps, I thought, as I enviously regarded the families picnicking alongside the stream, that is the key to it all, the joyful simplicity with which the pilgrims pass back and forth from their solemn entreaties to the inert Christ in the church to the boisterous conviviality in the rapidly flowing stream. For a single, all too brief moment, I understood, and then moved away to buy souvenirs for friends and relatives.

59. At Plaza Las Américas
(October 17, 1979)

Plaza Las Américas is the biggest shopping center on the island. At the time I wrote this column the place was just ten years old. To my surprise, this column brought in several indignant responses from readers, who suggested that if I was critical of shopping centers, perhaps I was a communist.

I went to Plaza Las Américas last Saturday afternoon and everyone there was under 15, either wearing braces or wanting a haircut. The real shock, however, was how garish, useless, and phony everything looked. I admit I hadn't been around any shopping center in the metropolitan area for rather a long time, since the only sensible place one should spend any loose change is in a bookstore. Still, I treasured memories of ample, air-conditioned spaces where one met long unseen acquaintances and chatted about the cosmos. I thought it would be a friendly gesture towards the human race to go into Plaza Las Américas and look at a price tag or two.

Well, I imagine that unless you really have to get something, the best thing is to leave such places on a Saturday afternoon to the hordes of eleven- year-olds determined to stake out some territory in the world for themselves. The current decor at the Plaza is something half way between the Wizard of Oz and Star Wars, but that doesn't necessarily please the intermediate generation. People and dummies are dressed so exactly alike that you keep brushing past the first and apologizing to the latter, which is all right, because at least they don't come back at you with some wise remark.

The public address system keeps telling Pepito that his mother is waiting for him by the fountain, and some guards with walkie-talkies importantly saunter by, assuring some hoarse superior that they have got right the description of "them." A pasty smell of pizza pervades the promenade. There are too many lights, signs, and exhibits, and even the two bookshops are so crammed with merchandise that one is discouraged from browsing. You begin feeling that some hidden machine has totaled up the money you have in your pocket and is sending a word to the Wicked Witch of the West that you aren't seriously contemplating a purchase.

And yet, as the advertisement says, this is the real "plaza" of Puerto Rico today, where people from Juncos meet their cousins from Las Piedras and talk about the latest wedding in the family. How they manage to gossip amidst so much noise and hurrying and emptying of wallets is a mystery, probably akin to the aspiration of having fun elbowing your way through the sweltering crowd in the *patronales* (your town's patron saint's feast). People really seem to be enjoying themselves. They compare prices, they give and receive tips on bargains, and they consume huge quantities of crusty food and over-iced refreshments. No one seems to mind the absurdities of the decorations or the alienating noises. They go to the fountain as if it were a real waterfall in the mountains of Utuado, and they stand there, gaping at it, or even, for a single instant, reflecting that there are better things in life than carrying around a shopping bag on a sultry afternoon.

But shopping has become entertainment. To buy somehow is to gain fulfillment. I imagine that there are people who can't think of anything else to do on a Saturday. Their longing wouldn't be to understand, or to share, or to create, but just to hear that cash register ring, and accumulate something else, some cheap imitation bibelot to show less fortunate neighbors in Comerío, some bauble to make one's house in Caguas look different.

Here one feels out of place. This is a temple whose devotees tolerate no idle sightseeing. One is intruding upon the musings of the serene old lady who lovingly fingers that fake marble tabletop. One shouldn't spy on that young mother who is almost playing with the dolls in the toy gallery. So one goes away empty-handed, having failed to remember why one went in the first place. It's like coming out of St. Patrick's Cathedral without having lighted a candle or said a prayer.

60. Grandpa's Story
(November 29, 1979)

*I got so much flak for the previous column that I had to write this one.
One of the letters to the editor suggested I was a grumpy grandfather (I
was 38 then), so I assumed the role.*

"Tell us a Christmas story," the children said, hoping the old man
would lose his ill temper.

"Now what would you be wanting a Christmas story for?" grumbled the old man. "None of you writes letters anymore to the Three
Kings."

"It's because it's that time of the year again," said the older girl; "in
December one tells Christmas stories."

"Well, prepare me a *pocillo* of coffee to help me over the rough
parts," said the old man, "and I'll tell you about the time governor
Romero went to Jayuya."

"Oh, not a political story," protested the child. "You know that in
December one should not talk about politicians."

"That's a new law to me," said the old man, "but since you don't
want to hear that story, I guess I'll have to talk about God. Well, listen carefully. Back in the times of Spain, one afternoon, when all the
men had been paid at the hacienda store, there appeared a strange
man selling eyeglasses in the barrio."

"My friends," he said, "these are not ordinary eyeglasses. These are
tinted glasses—blue, green, red, purple, yellow, any color you want.
Whoever uses these glasses will see things as they really are."

"But who wants to see things as they really are?" guffawed Andrés,
the foreman. "One drinks rum not to see things as they really are."

"Want to try a pair?" asked the hawker.

162

"No charge for trying, I guess," said Andrés.

The hawker handed over a pair of gray-tinted glasses and Andrés put them on. "Just as I expected," he said. "The owner will sell those steers before they are fat enough."

"You mean you see the future?" asked the field hands who had gathered around him.

"He is not getting a right price for those steers," said the foreman and took the glasses off.

"Do you want to buy the glasses?" asked the hawker.

"Not me," said Andrés. "One gets angry enough with the things one sees every day, let alone pay to see what one cannot help."

"Anybody else wants to try a pair?" asked the hawker.

"I'll try them," said José, the coffee winnower. The hawker handed him a pair of orange-tinted glasses, and he put them on. "Oh, that is beautiful," he said. "That is the nicest thing I ever saw."

"What is it, what is it?"

"I have seen her," said José; "she is singing while she washes the clothes by the river outside town."

"Do you want to buy the glasses?" asked the hawker.

"Oh, no, I cannot afford them," said José. "I must save every *real* so that we can get married by next Patron Saint's Day.

"Well, does anyone else want to try the glasses?" asked the hawker. "I'll give a chance to just one more person."

All wanted to be that one last person, but the hawker selected Rosenda, the cook from the big house. He handed her a pair of black-tinted glasses. She put them on and walked a few yards away from the crowd.

"What do you see, Rosenda?"

The little cook did not answer but seemed intent on gazing at the distance.

"Do you see a husband in your future, Rosenda?"

"Rosenda, is he handsome?"

"Tell us, Rosenda, when will he come for you?"

But Rosenda all the while was crying. The hawker came to get the glasses from her and he asked if she would buy them. "Oh, please," said Rosenda, "just a little bit more. I saw the Virgin with the child in Bethlehem and the ass and the ox. The child was sleeping, and he looked so happy, cuddled in his mother's arms."

"Do you want to buy the glasses?" asked the hawker.

"But I can't," said Rosenda. "I sent my savings to my sister, who had to take her child to the hospital in Ponce, and I must send some money again next week. He is my godchild."

"Then I must take the glasses away," said the hawker.

"But please," said Rosenda, "please. I'll pay you a bit every week, don't take the glasses away."

"Sorry," said he hawker, "but these glasses must be paid up all at once, or they lose their virtue."

Rosenda returned the glasses to him and sighed. "It is true—one sees things as they really are. And if I weren't poor I could have bought those glasses and would have seen the Virgin as often as I wanted."

The old man finished the *pocillo* of coffee. "And that's the story?" asked the older girl.

"That's the story," said the old man. "The poor can never afford to see what they want to see most."

"But nothing happens," said the child indignantly. "You have told a story in which nothing happens. Not a single person bought the glasses."

"Things happen here and here," said the old man pointing to his heart and head. "These are the only places where they really happen. You don't have to buy anything for something to happen."

But the child was wondering whether at Plaza las Américas they had such glasses.

61. Teaching Methods at the University of Puerto Rico
(December 13, 1979)

The fundamental mistake made at Puerto Rican universities over the last 20 years has been the assumption that the composition of the student body could be changed without changing teaching methods.

Over the past 20 years the University of Puerto Rico has mushroomed. From being a small, two-campus entity with several thousand students, it has become a giant institution that has added to the sites at Río Piedras and Mayaguez campuses at Humacao, Arecibo, Cayey, Ponce, Bayamon, Aguadilla, Carolina, and Utuado. The student body has grown eightfold, and the university's budget is bigger than that of the governments of independent nations in the New World.

As a result of this growth, and with the parallel growth of Catholic University, the Interamerican University, and other institutions, a university education in Puerto Rico is no longer the privilege of a professional elite. There is hardly a street in San Juan that doesn't have one or two university students. Scholarships, better opportunity grants, liberal loans, and other types of funding have made it possible for any high school graduate, with the capacity and determination of doing so, to obtain a university diploma.

The availability of the same resources has encouraged thousands of our students to seek their degrees in American universities. Many of them continue their professional training or graduate studies in the States, and not a few remain there once they are finished. Families that 20 years ago used to send their sons and daughters to Río Piedras now send them to Yale or Princeton.

This increased access to university education here and in the States is one of the principal achievements in recent times about which we ought to feel proud. It is now possible for great numbers of our people born in poverty to be able, through a university degree, to join the ranks of professionals.

When frustrated, however, this aspiration has become a source of bitterness for many university students who have had to drop out or who are about to get a degree that doesn't turn out to be the key to success. The university hasn't been what they were led to expect. It hasn't been much different from high school, except, perhaps, that one has more time on one's hands. There are classes at which a professor drones on, giving out data, formulas, or reflections; there are exams at which students are expected to return the same; and there are one or two papers or projects that some overzealous teacher assigns. For science majors there are the dull, dutifully spent hours in the laboratory; for education majors the exasperation of having to listen to a veteran public school teacher boast about personal teaching methods or the drudgery of having to do the work for him or her.

What university life means for many of such students is not the intellectual give-and-take or the adventure of discovering books in the library, but the gossip in the corridors, the games, movies, parties, the afternoons in which one escapes from the university to go to a beach or a shopping center. For these students, the university classroom, the professors' offices, and the libraries are places of torture, mutual deception, and boredom. Thus the university is not fulfilling for those students its proper function.

Many faculty members will say that such students do not belong in the university. But the truth is that many of those students arrived in the first year with a great deal of enthusiasm and a desire to study hard. Throughout their years at the university, however, they became disillusioned. Many of the classes were straight lectures, in which one could ask questions but didn't get a chance to express a personal insight. In classes in which there were discussions, the teacher imposed his own opinions, crushing with ridicule those who ventured to say something different. For exams one had to memorize definitions and data, because the teachers had little time to correct anything but multiple choice or fill-in-the-blank exams. And so education at the university seemed merely the process in which one satisfied one's elders that one had listened to them attentively.

Admittedly the experience of these disillusioned students was much broader. They also encountered brilliant teachers who uncovered for them brand new lines of thought or fired them with momentary enthusiasm for personal research or individual projects. But then the skills and resources those students brought with them didn't allow them to keep pace with these brilliant teachers. And what was more, these exceptional teachers seemed to think that reading 800 pages a week was easy for someone who had never had to read more than 20, or that one could read in English as easily as in Spanish. The teachers assumed that the students caught allusions to books they had never read, or that they could recognize a formula that they had seen once or twice. It was no use registering for courses with such teachers; you had to drop out or stand the chance of getting a bad mark.

Thus the universities of Puerto Rico have become giant mills, full of much sound and not a little fury, and in danger of signifying to our society little more than diploma factories. Teaching methods at the university level must be revised. It makes little sense to say that one is teaching young people to think for themselves when all that one requires from them is to memorize facts for so-called objective exams. And this revision of teaching methods is something that has to be done not by $100-a-day experts flown in from Carterland, but by the university faculties themselves. Inevitably questions will be raised about conditions of work, teaching loads, teaching assistants, and library resources, but those questions are not alien to but part and parcel of the problem of a deteriorating university education.

62. On Shoes as Flowers
(May 22, 1980)

On April 30, 1980, Luis Muñoz Marín, founder of the Popular Democratic Party and governor of Puerto Rico for 16 years (1948-1964), died. I accompanied the funeral processionl, which left old San Juan in the morning and arrived in Barranquitas at the end of the day. There was a massive outpouring of sentiment.

"When the old *jíbaros* from Orocovis arrived with flowers in their hands, that's when it hit me."

We had been talking about the immense tribute to Muñoz on the day of his funeral, and my socialist friend, born in Barranquitas, was describing to me how he had felt.

"They were not the kinds of flowers one buys, but the kind one cuts with one's own hands, '?*cruz de malta*,' ?*amapolas*.? The old people from Orocovis, walking into Barranquitas with bunches of flowers in their hands, that is something to remember."

I nodded, understanding what he was trying to say. Such things had their own way of happening. Another friend, Luis Agrait, told me about the following incident: "People tossed flowers on the hearse all along the way. But at a point between Cayey and Aibonito, an old lady ran barefooted towards the funeral procession and put her shoes on the hearse."

One could picture it, the Sunday shoes amidst the flower shops' carnations. It made one think. We have learned too many rites, too many gestures from dubbed films on television. But on exceptional occasions, such as the day of don Luis' funeral, the capacity to act spontaneously as a people surfaces and surprises everyone.

What one will always retain about that memorable day will not be the programmed events, solemn and impressive as they were, but what each unrehearsed knot of people, of its own accord, did along the way from San Juan to Barranquitas. It was a satisfying paradox that our day of mourning should have the exhilarating quality of a national celebration. The inconsistencies, the contrasts, the lack of uniformity, the monotonous comments one could hear along the way—all worked themselves together into a brilliant, intriguing mosaic of Puerto Rican character.

If one had thought that the city of San Juan had become too cynical to express one emotion simply, one had to see not just the staid, song-punctuated escort down Fortaleza Street, nor even the patricians of Miramar, standing at attention on their sidewalks, but the people from the *urbanizaciones* (subdivisions) alongside Highway One, with their radios and water coolers and beach umbrellas, intoning the songs one had judged they were too sophisticated to sing. They had filtered onto the road since mid-morning, until they had barely left the one necessary lane; and the sun they only courted on the beaches made them sweat in a proletarian fashion that was becoming for the occasion. With one hand they waved goodbye to an era, and with the other they held on firmly to the bright-eyed children whose innocent questions must have stung more than the noontime sun.

San Juan could achieve the elegance of simplicity easily, but along the road to Caguas one could see that there were people who had remembered in time the days they went barefoot, and like the characters from a novel that Enrique Laguerre never got to write, they had dashed out of their cement certitudes in curlers and half-buttoned shirts, with their ears attached to the radios that described to them what they were looking at. They sang, too, but there were the sudden tears of realization that what had been scheduled as a historic event could also mark a personal loss. The nearer one got to Caguas, the more articulate this raw, new Puerto Rico became, until on the Caguas bypass, as the funeral motorcade crawled over the roses, the people began sticking their heads into the escort cars, asking for mementos, asking for something that could be folded inside the pages of the brand-new family bibles.

Caguas was too tangled up in conflicting emotions and loyalties, too much the brand new city that has yet to tell apart what must be packaged and what wells up from the heart. Naranjito, Comerío, Gurabo, and San Lorenzo had come to crowd its overpasses, so that it was not as a single people but as a babel of sentiments that the valley saw the funeral procession ride on. One wondered if they would ever understand, or if one day they would buy encyclopedias to make sure that what they had seen had happened.

In Cayey, however, the sobriety of sentiment that used to mark the mountains asserted itself. The crowds had the solemnity that greeted Our Lady of the Assumption when in the old days she would come out of the church to review her *jíbaros* alongside the plaza. For occasions such as this one, old *cayeyanos* still wear panama hats, which are removed, row upon row, for the dead one, for the family, in respect. One would treasure more the silences of Cayey than the songs of Caguas, except that the contrast was not that neat, and the massive turnout precluded any single kind of tribute from being typical.

From then on it was the people from the mountains, lined all the way to Barranquitas, crying, waving, singing: *Tu serás el pájaro pinto.*

Their hand-made signs deficient in orthography, their flags and banners, the old, decades-old pictures of Muñoz, the stretch of road on which there were flowers on every tree, the bell tolled by a girl outside a country chapel, the incredible dignity of our mountain people that no actor can feign, so that a drunkard in Aibonito could outstare his would-be scoffers—that was beauty which belies all the Cassandra-like omens of cultural disintegration. The arrival at Barranquitas itself, of course, belongs to the anthologies. But if a lady between Cayey and Aibonito put her shoes as flowers on don Luis' hearse, how can one give up the effort to serve, as he did, such a people?

63. Scholarship in Puerto Rico
(June 19, 1980)

One of the handicaps under which any Puerto Rican who engages in research labors is the lack of understanding which our general public has for scholarly endeavors. It's not just the caricature of the scientist or the academic figure that popular TV programs perpetuate (why don't they caricature sportsmen or bankers?). It's the bland presupposition that research has nothing significant to contribute to our society, since any significant advance in any discipline is made in the States or in Europe anyway. A scholarly researcher, therefore, is someone eccentric, out of touch with ordinary reality, and a parasite who is perpetually asking for funds to look into irrelevant problems.

Even our academic societies, supposedly dedicated to the advancement of learning, prefer to listen to the well-mannered lawyer or priest who can speak with well-rounded phrases about the same old questions with the same old data than to be exposed to the abrasive university professor, who challenges old platitudes with fresh evidence. The supposedly cultured elite prefers general works in English to specialized books in Spanish. An educated man is one who can recite the genealogy of the English monarchs but is above knowing how much a slave used to cost in the San Juan market last century.

One of the results of such a discouraging perspective is that many of our brighter university graduates are choosing to stay in the United States rather than return to Puerto Rico and face minimal research facilities and a hostile environment. This is particularly true of scientists, to the point that qualified university teachers in some disciplines are hard to retain.

Now, why is it that there is such low esteem for scholarship in Puerto Rico? Maybe our educational system, like in so many other

171

things, is to blame. The student is not encouraged to find out things for himself, but rather to repeat, to the last iota, what has been taught in the classroom. The idea that a discipline is in process, and that one can be part of the discovery effort, is not stressed. Learning is just the operation by which the student assimilates what is known. Research skills are not developed. The public high school teacher who assigns term papers is considered a fool who gives himself an extra load of work. In any case he may condemn his students to frustration, since the school library is likely to be deficient and a municipal library nonexistent.

At the university level the student faced with crowded laboratory facilities or outdated library resources will be further discouraged by a testing system that measures "objective" knowledge by means of multiple choice, fill-in-the-blanks, and even true-or-false exams. The atmosphere of free inquiry and discussion that should characterize centers of higher learning is poisoned by cheap political slogans and instant dogmatism. Students who do original research find few outlets for publication and discussion of their work. Monolithic programs, crammed with required courses, do not allow for enough electives to suit specialized interests.

First-generation university graduates experience the pressure of their families, who can't understand why some should continue studying after receiving a bachelor's degree, especially if there is a job available. In fields such as law and business administration, where so much research should be done in Puerto Rico, the professions offer little inducement for postgraduate study. Success is measured by money made readily in the first years of professional work. The Chamber of Commerce and other civic groups honor salesmen, but not researchers in business management. It is a country in which boxers and beauty queens have readier access to the media to speak about social issues than sociologists.

So our young scholars drift toward the States; can you blame them? Until we learn to appreciate the challengers who can provoke a break with so much mediocrity and stagnation, we will continue deriving our wisdom from jaded politicians and charlatan astrologers.

Part VIII

Paris and Back

64. Monaco! Monaco!
(Letter from Paris, June 27, 1980)

In June 1980, there was a debate about whether Puerto Rican athletes should compete in the Moscow Olympics. In the end only the Boxing Federation opted to go.

Last Saturday, while walking towards the Bibliothèque Nationale, I ran into some 25 or 30 youngsters on the Rue de Rivoli. They were carrying red and white flags, shouting at the top of their lungs, and every now and then setting off fireworks. It was too early in the morning for it to be a

student demonstration and the wrong part of the city for a labor picket. A police car followed them along, but the officer had the bland expression that authorities here seldom exhibit at political marches.

Finally I caught on that what the exuberant marchers were shouting was "Monaco, Monaco!" and that they were indeed citizens of that sovereign state invading Paris for the "coupe de France," the championship soccer match against Orléans. The scene was reminiscent of *The Mouse That Roared*, the 1950's British comedy about a small European duchy that declares war on the United States in the hope of being defeated and receiving aid. But, of course, there was nothing defeatist in these belligerent Monaguesque youngsters set on taking on France. In fact, Monaco was the favorite team, and Orléans the underdog, and much to the chagrin of the French, who resent losing at anything, Monaco won that night.

Although it is the kind of thing one would never tell the French, I found myself hoping that Monaco would win the soccer match. Sports seem the appropriate terrain on which small nations can deflate the arrogance of big ones. To see the descendants of the 12th-century Mediterranean pirates of Monaco marching with flags unfurled through the most elegant section of Paris at the outrageous hour of nine in the morning did one's heart a great deal of good. It didn't compensate for Napoleon's armies trampling on most of the European capitals, but it reminded one that, after all, the haughty French were vulnerable to the fortunes of a spinning ball.

The incident reminded me of the ridiculous debate about participation in this year's Olympic games in Moscow. Anyone with the least sense of historical perspective knows that in 10 or 20 years Jimmy Carter will be judged harshly for his attempt to disrupt the Olympic games to save his presidential candidacy. The effort to infect international sports with short-range political motivations discredits a presidency that hasn't been able to rally the American people around common national goals. Carter boycotts the Olympic games as a punishment for the Soviet occupation of Afghanistan in the same way that teachers penalize children by giving them bad marks because they happen to disagree with the political stances of the children's parents. Why didn't he forbid the delivery of goods that had already been contracted by American firms with the Soviet Union? Wasn't there the same kind of commitment to the Olympic games?

The real American response to the Olympic challenge should have been to go to Moscow and win. Perhaps, of course, the results of last summer's Spartakiad in Moscow discouraged American analysts, who may have felt that the Soviets had trained so hard for the coming games that it would have been difficult for Americans to beat these athletes. But then the president should have been frank about the real reason for the boycott: "We aren't going because they are going to beat us." At least the Little League World championship organizers were as frank several years ago when they forbade the participation of Taiwan.

Here in Paris a few people know about the Puerto Rican Olympic Committee's wise resolution to allow individual sports federations to decide about participation in the Olympic games. The reaction is generally favorable; after all, except for Paraguay and a couple dozen other dictatorships, most of the Western world has refused to see in Carter's boycott anything but a political ploy. What, of course, remains disturbing is the stupid way in which a few right-wing agitators have tried to discredit our Olympic committee's stance with spots on the radio and letters to the editor. Why should we in Puerto Rico be so isolated from public opinion in the rest of the world as to suffer such fanatical pressure?

The Pope himself is known to be cool to the Olympic boycott. The instance of the 1936 Berlin Olympics, so maladroitly popularized by sports columnist Red Smith in the States, if anything serves as a reminder that sportsmen from free countries can show a dictatorial host country what free men and women can accomplish in sports competition.

What the Puerto Rican basketball team should do is to go to Russia and march, with flags unfurled, down the streets of Moscow and then go on to win the gold medal. That would be our response to Afghanistan.

65. Alcuin or Merlin
(June 30, 1980)

It is one of the enduring attractions of Paris that one can always stroll to a different secondhand bookstore and spend a peaceful half an hour there looking at publications discarded or left behind by previous generations. The other day, browsing through the immense repertoire of books in English at Shakespeare and Co., James Joyce's old refuge near Saint-Julien-le-Pauvre on the Left Bank, I found an old classic, Eleanor Shipley Duckett's *Alcuin, Friend of Charlemagne*. It is the kind of biography everyone refers to—"for Alcuin, of course, there is Duckett's book"—but never seems to get around to reading. So I bought it and put it by the bedside, and much to my surprise I found that it pushed back my sleeping time. Duckett had been so skillful in quoting her subject's letters and identifying his correspondents that when I finished reading it, I felt I had almost met Alcuin personally.

As head of Charlemagne's palace school at Aachen and as abbot of Saint Martin de Tours, the Northumbrian Alcuin helped launch one of the most significant cultural movements in Western history—the so-called Carolingian renaissance. It was partly by his doing that the works of ancient pagan and Christian authors were saved from disappearance. He was responsible for the liturgical aggiornamento of his day, helping establish, among other things, the custom of singing the creed after the Gospel on Sundays, and encouraging the celebration of All Saints'Day (whose eve, Halloween, has become in our times the delight of children everywhere). He encouraged Charlemagne to assist popes Hadrian I and Leon III, thus helping to weld the thousand-year alliance between northern emperors and the popes. His disciples, spread throughout Western Europe, kept alive the torch of learning he had transmitted to them, multiplying the centers of study at a time when the Carolingian empire was beginning to collapse.

Never canonized by the Church, Alcuin had nonetheless a reputation for holiness and miracle working throughout the Middle Ages. Medieval anthologists looked back at him as the wise old man who was the repository of ancient learning, the authority who could back up liturgical usages of doctrinal traditions. He became legendary, one of the two sage advisers of great kings. The other one was Merlin, to whom even more marvelous powers were attributed, probably because he never existed.

Now, it is a striking fact that in our popular culture, which knows the early Middle Ages more through *Prince Valiant* of the Sunday comics than through scholars like Duckett, the shadowy Arthurian Merlin of Camelot should be more real than the articulate Alcuin of Aachen. One has an image of Merlin, with flowing beard and pointed cap: one finds it confirmed in T.H. Stone's *The Once and Future King* or in C.S. Lewis's *That Hideous Strength.* Merlin sees the future and is a specialist in pyrotechnics; as in Mark Twain's *A Connecticut Yankee in King Arthur's Court*, one never trusts him altogether because there's a Celtic strain in him that yearns, beyond Roman law and Christian doctrine, for magic and midnight rituals in the forest. King Arthur, without Merlin, is a babe in the woods; Merlin, without Arthur, is the harsh druid dooming the oncoming of the axe.

This image, built up by medieval romance and modern tract, appeals to us to the degree that we like to envisage the past both as mysterious and as peopled by simple and passionate figures. For King Arthur's Britain, Merlin, Morgan-le-Fay, and the Holy Grail take care of the mystery part, while Arthur, Lancelot, and Guinevere are almost straight out of Ibsen.

Twelfth-century medieval schoolmen, once they set themselves seriously to the task of systematizing learning, had, in a sense, to choose between Merlin and Alcuin. These were the two legendary wise men who were the popular models of learning at that time. One had never existed but had a real enough life in the songs of troubadours; the other one appeared in glosses and anthologies and collections of letters that monks began to recopy around this time. Learning could be recondite but prodigiously impressive, as in Merlin, or it could be stubbornly prosaic and charmingly homely, as in Alcuin. The Merlin of romance was a solitary figure linking knowledge and power; the Alcuin of tradition sought in fellowship the knowledge of God.

And medieval learning hesitated between these two profane models of wisdom and encyclopedic knowledge, and sometimes it leaned to the fanfare of arcane formulas, as in the case of the alchemists, and sometimes it besought in tears a higher knowledge, like Bonaventure, and pounded the table, like Aquinas, when he found a telling logical argument. But it eventually became clear that Merlin's knowledge was a fantasy and Alcuin's a source of scholastic learning; that knowledge could not be obtained by drawing magic circles or mixing Oriental powders, but was something that could be attained systematically by observation and deduction. Above all, it became clear that knowledge was not the privilege of the initiated but the birthright of all those who had the talent to attend disputations at the universities. It was Alcuin who had prevailed over Merlin, the teacher over the wizard.

66. A Weekend Night in Paris
(July 9, 1980)

Strolling down the Boulevard Saint-Germain between Cluny and the Cafe de Fiore on a weekend summer evening, one is always surprised by the vivaciousness of the throng of people and by the diversity of the entertainments offered by amateurs on the sidewalk. There are jugglers; mimes; fire-eaters; violinists; hawkers of woodcarvings, of painted miniatures, and of exotic apparel and toys; singers; and guitar, bagpipe, and clavichord players. At any one time you can hear German, English, Spanish, Arabic, Italian, and Portuguese spoken under the pervading hum of French. There are young people in faded jeans from everywhere, with packs on their shoulders and brand new maps in their hands. There are shy, middle-aged couples from every province in the world, and knowledgeable old boulevardiers, seeking a favorite spot at a cafe they used to frequent in their student days, before the world went foolish.

In a city like Paris there is never any question on a Saturday night about what the young can do after the movies. Go to the Latin Quarter and the boulevard Saint-Germain, of course. There you can buy pastry at some North African shop, or sip a beer at a cafe, or slip into a circle of people watching a strongman break out of chains, or even join a group singing ballads at Saint-André-des Arts. Or you can watch a three-minute comedy improvised by student actors before the Deux Magots or a trained goat climb a ladder, or listen to capitalism discussed on a street corner. No two nights on the boulevard Saint-Germain are identical.

When you see so many people having a good time in a relatively simple way, your mind inevitably goes back to San Juan. For what does our capital city have to offer the young on a weekend night? The same police thrillers or horror movies chosen by distributors who go on the theory that the average I.Q. of our young people is 80 and their culture zero, the high-priced discotheques, or the furtively smoked "joint." "There is nothing to do on a Saturday night; it's always the same." How many times has one heard that phrase?

Of course, there was the *placita* San José. Young people could go there, mill around, talk, listen to a guitar. But the reaction of the authorities was typical. Since some disturbances had occurred, since there were some justifiable complaints, then the young must be chased away. Break a few skulls, if necessary, but keep them away for good. The sledgehammer solution: look at the symptoms, not at the real problem.

"To understand the *placita* San Jose," a student told me last year, before the police converged on it, "you have to know that fellows and girls go there because they want to be part of something, they want to participate in something. There they are the scene, they are the act."

He proceeded to give me this instance: "One night a group of us were returning from some activity, and we decided to stop a minute at the *placita;* we had heard so much about it. One of the fellows had a guitar; he started strumming it, and we started singing, not too loud, a couple of religious songs. Just to pass the time, you see. And before we knew it, a whole group of kids had gathered around us. They wanted us to continue. Someone even thought we were going to preach to them, like the *catacumbas.* But, you see, they were just waiting there for something to happen, something in which they could participate, even if it were a religious thing."

Somehow government officials and civic groups have to understand that the needs of the young are not solved just by building them basketball courts and haranguing them about their important role in the future. You have to multiply the scene at the *placita* San Jose by 70 to understand the feeling of futility and tedium which too many of our young people nourish. The square at Adjuntas at 1 p.m. on a weekday afternoon, the basketball court at Utuado on a summer evening, the *cafetines* in Caguas on a Friday night—the examples are there for all to see.

Activities ought to be organized for and by the young during summertime. Town squares, parks, and community centers should be available for imaginative recreational activities that don't entail much bureaucratic supervision or budgetary investment. Civic groups should get off their perpetual rounds of self-congratulations and organize simple and attractive activities. The churches, which are ever foremost in moralizing about the decadent habits of the young. should pitch in and contribute solutions for a change. But above all, young people themselves should seize the initiative and change the recreational climate in Puerto Rico.

67. A College for Prison Inmates
(Letter from Paris, July 26, 1980)

Little did I imagine that ten years later I would be involved in such a venture.

If on a rainy Saturday afternoon you should chance to be in the Manuscripts Room of the Bibliothèque Nationale in Paris and you should request the consultation of Latin manuscript 9902 (but one can think of better ways of spending even a rainy afternoon in Paris), turn to the reverse side of folio 49. It is a 16th-century copy of an early 14th-century charter of king Philip V. Now, 16th-century hands are hard to read, and if you are accustomed to the easygoing ways of 13th-century amanuenses, you are apt to grumble about how the supposedly enlightened days of Francis I spelled a calamitous deterioration in handwriting. The scribes became all business, hardly sparing time for a capital letter here and there, and certainly disregarding those neat commas and periods that give so many welcome hints to readers of medieval manuscripts. But if you overcome these difficulties and tarry over the page, there appears on the verso of folio 49 a vignette of life under the last Capetians.

In his charter of 1318 Philip V tells a short story. His sister-in-law Clementine (the widow of Louis X) was passing through Laigny when she met a doleful procession. The local justiciar was escorting to execution by hanging a certain young man who had been found guilty of theft. But here were the village people, all tears, asking the ex-queen to intercede, and especially, the king states, "a certain young girl called Jeannette Ruffi, who was asking, with much weeping," that the young man in question be given in marriage to her. Well, what could the lady Clementine do in the circumstances but direct that the

184

young man be spared and released? So the king has to sit down and dictate this charter to the provost of Paris, certifying that the rights of high justice of the monastic authorities of Laigny are not in the least impaired by the queen's exercise of indulgence. And that at Laigny one took such matters seriously can be seen by the fact that two hundred years after the event they were copying down the charter on the local cartulary, in remembrance of the fact that their right to hang people had been recognized by the king of France.

Well, of course, good queen Clementine hadn't been arbitrary in acting in behalf of the anonymous young thief. Further south from Laigny, in the Laonnois, Jacques Foviaux has documented the unwritten custom that if on the hanging day of any condemned prisoner a woman asked for him in marriage, he would be spared. For it was one of the quirks of medieval justice that it was both exceptionally severe and sensationally merciful. They would condemn you to death for stealing a lamb (whence the English saying that you might as well be hanged for a sheep as for a lamb), but they would release you on the spot if a spinster requested you in marriage. Or it could happen to you as it did to some brash delinquents in 13th-century England, who were allowed to climb down from the gallows on condition that they became Templar knights in the crusader state of Jerusalem,

Apparently, knight service at Acre and marriage to a spinster were seen as desirable social services, which were suitable alternatives to capital punishment. A wife could always keep a spirited young man away from the neighbors' stock, and there was nothing like riding in the Syrian desert to help a young blade settle down in life. Imaginative solutions, no doubt, to what must have seemed in the 13th-century to be a mounting tide of criminality. But of course there were far too many hangings in proportion to the number of those spared.

In any case, there was no question of keeping people locked up for life. Justice was concerned with meting out a solution to the criminal's problem, as well as society's. A barbarous solution, no doubt, in the case of those condemned to death (for the death penalty, under all circumstances and in any age, is savage and inhumane). But a luminous way of handling those cases marked for mercy. You didn't just release someone, you gave him a role in life.

According to the statistics that are periodically released by police authorities throughout the Western world, more than half and sometimes even three fourths of petty crimes are committed by unemployed young people. They are sent to jail, they are paroled, they are still unemployed, and, to nobody's surprise, they wind up back in jail. One of the ironic aspects of so-called penal reform legislation, both in France and in Puerto Rico, is the expressed desire to focus on punishment rather than on rehabilitation as the object of sentencing. It is ironic, because there has seldom been any rehabilitation effort worth the name, either in France or in Puerto Rico. Young ex-convicts are likely candidates for jail, not because the penal system has been too mild with them, but because it has often deprived them of the last vestiges of role identity and personal dignity. They went to prison because they were persons who had disregarded the law, and in prison they become persons for whom the law has no regard.

The reform of the penal system is a priority that successive administrations adopt and none has successfully undertaken. It is often confused with building new prison facilities (which were badly needed) or with upgrading personnel (which is always commendable). But the convicts are left with the meager resources that remain once the budget for personnel and structures gobbles up most of the inadequate appropriations. For convicts in Puerto rico, there is very little professional training and only limited educational facilities.

Why not open, through the cooperation of the Justice Department and the University of Puerto Rico, a college at some commonwealth prison? The wags, of course, will scoff at the idea, as they are apt to do whenever getting a ready laugh is easier than turning out a solution to a human problem. But why can't such a program be undertaken, if not by the public sector, then by churches or civic groups? The cost? The paperwork? But a college so conceived doesn't have to run into the usual costs of a classical institution of higher education. A college with 80 or 100 students doesn't need a bureaucracy, and it could handle its administrative needs by drawing from the student body itself. And the teachers could be recruited from the multitude of retired professors who are eager to do something significant with their time.

It could be a worthwhile, imaginative experiment, which might open new horizons to lives spent in unworthy frustration.

68. Florencio Picó
(August 28, 1980)

My father, Florencio Picó, is turning 80 on Friday the 29th and the prospect does not please him much. He would prefer to be seventy-ten or perhaps *quatre-vingt*, as the French put it, four times twenty. Eighty sounds too imposing and for a person who likes to do things his own way, it's even a restraint. People somehow expect one to alter the rhythm of life, to sit down and tell stories to grandchildren, or to play dominoes. My father is not bent on such things. He reads the newspapers avidly, follows step by step the electoral campaign, and urges my mother, or anyone within reach, to ponder all the paragraphs in the press that he has underlined.

For him politics does not consist of that newfangled thing publicity people have concocted and whose object is to con votes out of trusting citizens with studied televised images. Politics for him is the art of governing well, not the knack of winning elections. A lifetime public servant who never ran for public office, he doesn't believe in weakening the government, no matter which party is in power. The government belongs to the public: the administration of public funds is a sacred trust, beyond the reach of party allegiances; the performance of public service is an exacting duty, which demands personal sacrifice. One may strive to oust a party from power, but to do so one will never cheapen the prestige of the government itself.

He belongs to an extraordinary generation of people who chose to serve anonymously for decades in the public agencies and other branches of government so that the Puerto Rican reality could be transformed. He has never forgotten the chaos and misery of the 1930's, the perpetual charade of sweet-tongued legislators touring the mountain towns in a round-robin competition to establish who had begged the most money from Washington.

As a Treasury Department inspector, he looked into enough municipal account books to be able to detect at a glance how unscrupulous politicians could direct public monies toward partisan purposes. Once, in the early thirties, he was summoned to Fortaleza by the governor, who wanted him to change an adverse report on some members of the Caguas municipal government. He refused to do so. His reputation for inflexibility grew with the years. Fellow Treasury employees would joke that on his desk there was a sign, *"Que pague!"*—have him pay—his consistent response to any effort to let someone off from paying duties or back taxes.

When Muñoz broke with the Liberals, my father followed him into what became the Popular Democratic Party. He devoted much of his free time to helping organize the party, and never swerved from personal loyalty to Muñoz. The new philosophy of government of the 1940's reflected many of his personal values. In the mid 1940's he became the first treasurer of the Aqueducts Authority, a post in which he served until his retirement in 1964. His enthusiasm for the development of the agency knew no bounds. A typical family outing would be a visit to a new project; he would examine the huge pipes, ask innumerable questions of whomever happened to be the caretaker, and explain to us how the water would be treated. We grew up hearing about bonds, blueprints specifications, and especially the annual report, that yearly ordeal that somehow changed the whole pace of life at home.

My father has always been a confirmed believer in education. He would scrutinize our report cards with the same care he used to bestow on the municipal account books of Dorado or Manatí, and one would have to explain, with full details, any mark short of an A. With the second generation, my nephews, he has been more liberal and allowed an occasional B+ to pass muster. But he has never accepted the shortcomings of a teacher as the explanation for a low mark. At home a teacher would always be held up as an object of respect, and education was considered one of the more esteemed professions. I suspect my father would have enjoyed teaching as a career;

actually, he taught high school in Guayama for some time in the early 1920's.

Or perhaps that is what he has been all the time, an educator, pausing here to instruct a casual acquaintance on how to fill out some papers for a government agency, or stopping there to explain to a life-long friend the third paragraph from the bottom in that speech printed on the back pages of *El Mundo.* My mother takes it all with a grain of salt. She listened to all his renderings of Muñoz speeches; she impishly suggests that he has not altogether convinced her this time about the respective merits of Hernán Padilla and Celeste Benitez [(mayoral candidates in 1980]; she suspects that, after all, Romero and Hernández Colón are friends. My father picks up the paper and opens it to the latest press interview: "It's all here," he says, "read what I have underlined: it's a philosophy of government that is involved."

69. A Guaguita Driver's Binge
(March 19, 1981)

In 1980 I had moved to barrio Caimito, then a semi-rural ward of San Juan. To go to the University every day I traveled on the guaguita, which is a 16-passenger van. Thus began my lifelong attachment to Caimito, which resulted in the book Vivir en Caimito (To Live in Caimito).

As soon as I got on the guaguita at 8:30 in the morning, I knew something was different. I sat on the *asiento de la muerte,* the seat in the second row that has nothing in front of it, so that in accidents the passenger seated there goes flying towards the windshield. The driver unsuccessfully invited a couple of young women to climb aboard, and, rebuffed, shrugged his shoulders and drove on. Then I noticed he smelled of rum.

At no moment during the ride to Río Piedras did he drive in an unsafe way or at an unusual speed. Nor were any of my fellow passengers concerned that we might have an accident. It's true, I didn't altogether forget that I was on the siege perilous, but I was sure that we were going to make it to the Río Piedras square without much trouble.

The driver was on the fourth day of celebrating the birth of his second son, and the fact that he had been drinking almost all night and had slept very little didn't in the least muddle his Homeric expression. The passengers contributed a chorus of "oohs" and "ahhhs" to his relating of his exploits, and a religiously minded middle-aged lady seated beside me interjected a running commentary culled from the elementary canon of middle-age morality.

"Since Saturday, I have spent all my savings, $700 in all. I filled up the guaguita with gas, so whatever I make on this trip, I'll spend it on drink."

"Ooh!"

"I have already bought and distributed among my passengers seven boxes of cigars. I paid someone $50 to drive me to Ponce and back."

"But why have someone drive you?" asked the religious lady.

"Because I'am always carrying passengers, day in and day out. So I wanted someone to take me instead, to feel the luxury of it. I had the money, I could afford it."

"Ahhh!"

"My brother-in-law painted the whole inside of my house for $100."

"Only for $100?"

"He stole the paint, so he just put in his labor, and I gave him enough to drink."

"Ooh!"

"You have to know how to take advantage of things," the driver said. "You have to enjoy life, to grab every good chance. Look at this. I bought from so-and-so $130 of food stamps for $100. He needed the money, and I grabbed the chance; that's the only way you can get ahead in life."

"But that—" said the religious lady, trying to give expression to her indignation. But the driver wouldn't give her the chance to sound off.

"The baby is coming today from the hospital, but the wife will be staying there until Friday."

"So you're going to give the baby rum instead of milk?"

"That might be a good idea. But my sister is taking care of him until Friday. And my mother-in-law has the other kid. I hope she doesn't spoil him."

"So you are going to keep drinking even though the baby is coming today?"

"Certainly," said the driver. "I am not through celebrating yet; not until the wife comes back."

"Those kids are going to take to drink if you keep showing them the way."

"They will drink when they get to be 15 whether I'm sober now or drunk. That's the way kids are. But let me tell you another story. You know so-and-so, the wife of X. Well, I was coming back from the square with her as my only passenger, because I wasn't going to sit there waiting for passengers to appear; it was the middle of the afternoon."

"You came back with only one passenger?"

"Right. This was on the first day. I tell her, 'Let's stop at the cafetín [bar] and drink one for the baby's health.' And she says, 'I'll have a pineapple juice, please.' Juice! Can you imagine? And she even wanted to plunk down her 40 cents for it. I was furious! Pineapple juice! She could have accepted at least a beer."

We got to the Río Piedras square, paid the fare, and got off. The religious lady was still shaking her head, and some of the passengers were saying, "Imagine, three more days."

It had been a long time since I had witnessed such an exuberant celebration of life.

70. Jorge Bauermeister
(July 23, 1982)

Having read the Sunday's gospel, I look at the expectant eyes of the congregation and start my homily. "My Uncle Jorge tells me the story of . . ." Immediately everyone's attention is riveted on the tale. My Uncle Jorge Bauermeister's stories about the old days in Cayey are an infallible means of effectively introducing a homily topic at the barrio chapel. There are stories of picaresque types and their ingenuity, of smart alecks, of clever answers and impossible escapades, of monumental naivete and outrageous brashness, all illustrating the wisdom and the wit of the *cayeyanos.*

A lifelong farmer, my uncle has seen the ups and downs of coffee planting, cattle raising, and truck farming in the mountains of Cayey. He is a stubborn individualist, one of the last farmers in the municipality. Every now and then I go hiking and visit him. While I sit on the porch, sipping my Aunt Laura's *parcha* juice, my uncle asks, "Did I tell you the story of don Cindo and the *espiritista?"*

"That's a new one."

"It happened that don Cindo's wife . . ."

One story leads to the next, and soon I have four or five stories for my Sunday masses. Then my uncle becomes serious: "How can we ever fix this country again after eight years of Romero?"

Needless to say, he has voted for the Popular Democratic Party (PDP) since 1940 and listens avidly to the political programs on the radio. But symptomatically, he is disenchanted with the present leadership's public relations approach to current issues. "What's right is right, and what's wrong, you've got to denounce it. Now take all those people with consultant fees. Do you think we have built this party over such a long period of time and struggled so hard and then have these people in San Juan live off Muñoz Marín's reputation? Ah, he wouldn't have stood for such goings on."

"You don't think the party leadership is sensitive about what the back country feels about the *batatas* [useless hired consultants]?"

"Well, they may be, but they solve everything with polls. When was the last time any of them listened to the people? They are too busy in meetings, figuring out how they are going to win the elections."

I am surprised at my uncle's emphasis on the need to return to "the spirit of 1940." And I wonder how widespread this feeling is among the party's pioneers. In recent years, there has been an unfortunate tendency in the PDP to take these rock bottom supporters for granted. Eager to garner the young urban vote, the party's tactics have been geared to creating an image of sophisticated urbanity for its leadership. The trouble is that that image doesn't mix well with the party's avowed purpose of exercising power in behalf of the downtrodden and destitute. Together with the simple, rural image has gone the zeal to organize the people so as to be able to help themselves. Don't the new leaders understand that the 1940 party was not seeking the proliferation of welfare programs, but rather the socialization of land and utilities and the restructuring of public priorities to give the working classes a voice in their own destiny?

Tampering with images of the PDP, publicists have attempted to "modernize" the party's appeal. But such tactics have yielded only short-term advantages. It is not images but ideas that the PDP needs. And unfortunately these are in short supply among hired campaign consultants. They can sell a political platform, but they don't construct one.

What holds the Popular Democratic Party together nowadays, beyond Muñoz' legacy, is the New Progressive Party. In the desire to regain power and displace their powerful rivals, all *Populares* stand together. But what people like my Uncle Jorge would like to know is what party program is going to be put into effect: a program of socioeconomic reconstruction or a program of distributing prebends and contracts in the style of the House of Representatives?

The PDP will know only too late how its credibility has been affected by the club of insiders that collects offices and fees. It's the very conception of politics that is at stake—whether the image is more important than the message, whether internal democracy can be sacrificed to the image itself. People like my Uncle Jorge feel that the New Progressive Party should be no looking glass for a party that claims to be different.

71. Time for a Change
(August 13, 1984)

There was an ongoing tussle between "old" and "new" historians. As a result of this column, I received a blasting response in El Mundo *from the then dean of Puerto Rican historians. I chose not to answer it but to write a history of Puerto Rico myself.*

The teaching of Puerto Rican history in our high schools and universities is still, by and large, in the grip of the traditional school of historiography that dominated the University of Puerto Rico's history department from the late 1940's to the late 1970's.

Even if it is *independentistas* or statehooders who may be teaching it at a given institution, the history taught still bears the imprint of Arturo Morales Carrión, Lidio Cruz Monclova, Ricardo Alegría, Aida Caro, Luis Manuel Díaz Soler, Labor Gómez Acevedo, and other researchers and teachers of the same period at the university.

What distinguished this entrenched school of Puerto Rican historians is a particular vision of the historical process in Puerto Rico and a particular notion of how to go about researching and writing it. Their platonic model of what Puerto Rico is incarnates itself in certain stages of our collective past.

The Puerto Rican Taíno Indian, the Puerto Rican African slave, the Puerto Rican Spanish settler are researched and portrayed in terms of what the model Puerto Rican should be. Their particular stories are told in terms of the history into which they are eventually to meld. No conflict is so severe, no particular trait so prevalent, no institution so foreign that it cannot eventually be subsumed into that finished product, the Puerto Rican identity.

Thus this traditional school plays down the history of our internal conflicts: the slave conspiracies, murders, and escapes; the brutality of the conquest of the Indians; and racial discrimination, economic exploitation, political turmoil, rampant criminality, and acute misery.

In eradicating or shunting aside most evidence of these phenomena, these worthy historians were probably acting under the impression that to offer Puerto Ricans a positive and homogenous image of their past, especially their past under Spanish dominion, one should not play up conflicts that after all had happened long ago and were forgotten. At the risk of projecting passivity on the past, they strove to elaborate a positive image of Puerto Rico, especially in comparison with the United States. The history of exploitation and of past struggles did not serve that purpose.

How successful their historiographical model has been can be measured by what the average Puerto Rican university graduate these days can state coherently about our collective past:

- That the English and the Dutch tried to wrest San Juan away from Spain.
- That there was slavery here, but it wasn't as bad as in other places and in any case did not leave a heritage of racial discrimination.
- That, frustrated by a long wait for special laws, some Puerto Ricans plotted against Spain, staged an uprising in Lares, and failed, since they did not have the backing of the general population.
- That although autonomy was granted in the end by Spain, Puerto Rico became involved in the final phase of the Spanish-American war, and thus American troops "came" to Guánica.
- That conditions thereafter improved to the degree that Puerto Ricans learned the virtues of the ballot box and legislated away disease, ignorance, and poverty.

This is all the history that most educated people in Puerto Rico care to know, and burdened with so little baggage they can happily inform their North American fellow citizens that Puerto Rico doesn't have much of a history.

What worries one most about that crass model, with which the traditional historians are as uncomfortable as the new ones, is that in it historical causation is simplified to the limit. Most things happened because external forces imposed them on us; what we have done on our own has been possible because external forces permitted it.

Thus the initiative ever reverts to the outsiders, and it is no surprise: you can count proper names in any of our traditional history books and find there more names of foreigners than of Puerto Ricans.

If the history of Puerto Rico has been taught as the history of what outsiders have done in Puerto Rico, what surprise is there in reading contemporary columnists who actually seem to believe that the solution to our problems rests on Washington's initiatives?

Thus, ironically, the history that was written to induce Puerto Ricans to have a positive image of themselves has resulted in some Puerto Ricans' vision of our historical process as being manufactured and modeled from outside.

72. Say Yes to People
(June 2, 1987)

Dile No a las Drogas, el Bobo de los Bobos *was a huge publicity campaign that was launched to eradicate the use of addictive drugs. The tendency was to represent addicts in a demeaning way. I had come in contact with people who were troubled by this campaign, even to the extent of considering taking their own lives.*

The current campaign against drug addiction runs the risk of becoming a crusade against drug addicts. No one is in favor of drug addiction and everyone is conscious of all the social ills that derive from it and from its criminalization. But the blitz in the media, like the New Progressive Party's advertising in the 1980 campaign, has reached its counterproductive stage. When youngsters start mimicking the ads, you know saturation has been reached.

Worse than saturation. This campaign against drug addiction has borrowed its strategy from some of the most reactionary approaches to the rehabilitation of addicts. By demeaning and ridiculing the addict you may attempt to prevent others from joining his ranks, but it is a poor service to society to stigmatize a minority and to render addicts as social outcasts.

Imagine for a moment that a campaign against alcoholism was launched by some well-meaning institution. Would you care to see look-alikes of your husband or wife treated in ads against alcoholism the way addicts of cocaine or heroin are treated? Would you enjoy seeing a prominent singer next to a tomb reminding you of the evils of having a couple of drinks after work every day? Addiction to alcohol probably causes more heart and liver diseases in Puerto Rico than the smoking of marijuana. But those solemn and civic-minded business leaders who so righteously back the campaign against marijuana would be peeved if an ad even suggested that they are addicted to those daily shots of gin after a hard day's work.

When someone falls into the grip of drugs, the feeling of rejection from society he or she may already entertain is reinforced by the reaction of the family to his or her drug problem. The current campaign tends to reinforce those patterns of rejection. By lowering the self-esteem of the addict and by presenting him or her as an idiot, you only succeed in pushing him further into the embrace of drugs and of the drug user's peer group. And by presenting marijuana as being on the same level as hard drugs, you encourage a wide group of youngsters who have tried it to experiment with the hard drugs. Represent people dying of marijuana use and your credibility is gone. Keep giving marijuana smokers a stigma, and soon they will perceive themselves as addicts.

Alcohol and tobacco are addictive, and yet we don't treat victims of that kind of addiction as idiots. If drug consumption is illegal, it is because it is addictive, and society wants to protect its members from such harm. But it is usually youngsters who have other kinds of problems who turn to drugs for a respite from their troubles. Getting them off drugs does not solve their original problems. They know it.

Why not take a more positive approach to the problem of drug addiction? Instead of locking up young addicts in institutions where they may be brainwashed, why not develop some creative programs of community service in which they will develop a positive view of themselves? Why can't they make videos of their communities, edit barrio newspapers, participate in photography competitions, enter chess and checkers tournaments, stage local pet shows, record interviews with old timers, form bicycle clubs, do volunteer work in hospitals, train as junior members of the Civil Defense or as ecology watchdogs, create public opinion surveys, learn veterinary skills, clean the litter off beaches, become volunteer firemen, or participate in reforestation efforts? There is a hidden talent in each person that is not always discovered. Why don't the churches and civic groups do more to help youngsters find their own talents?

The criminalization of drug addiction has pushed the young into a legal morass. In the 16th century they used to treat dissenters in the same fashion. We might yet be witnessing the beginning of another inquisitorial age. But there is still time to realize that the problem is not drug addiction but rather what drives young people to drug addiction. It is institutions, mentalities, and practices that make of them objects and discard them when they don't measure up to role expectations.

CPSIA information can be obtained
at www.ICGtesting.com
Printed in the USA
FFOW01n1744050516
23797FF